THE TASTE OF OUR TIME

Collection planned and directed by

ALBERT SKIRA

BIOGRAPHICAL AND CRITICAL STUDIES

BY

JACQUES LASSAIGNE

Translated by Stuart Gilbert

LAUTREC

SKIRA

Title Page:
The Salon in the Rue des Moulins (detail), 1894.
Musée d'Albi.

✶

© by Edition d'Art Albert Skira, 1953.

✶

Distributed in the United States by
THE WORLD PUBLISHING COMPANY
2231 West 110th Street - Cleveland 2, Ohio.

CHRONOLOGICAL SURVEY

1864 **Birth at Albi, November 24, of Henri, son of Alphonse de Toulouse-Lautrec-Monfa and Adèle Tapié de Céleyran.**

1867 Paris World's Fair. Death of Baudelaire and Ingres. Birth of Pierre Bonnard.

1868 Degas begins to go to the theater for his subjects.

1869 Renoir and Monet work at Bougival. Birth of Henri Matisse.

1870 Franco-Prussian War. Proclamation of the Third Republic.

1871 The Paris Commune. Birth of Georges Rouault.

1873 **Coming to Paris with his family, Lautrec begins his studies at the Lycée Fontanes (today Lycée Condorcet), where his schoolfellow and bosom friend is Maurice Joyant, later his biographer. A delicate boy, he follows treatments at Amélie-les-Bains. Precocious talent for drawing.**

1874 First Group Exhibition of the Impressionists in Nadar's galleries, Boulevard des Capucines; Manet abstains.

1875 Death of Corot.

1878 **In two successive accidents, at Albi in 1878 and some months later during a course of treatment at Barèges, Lautrec breaks both thighs. This infirmity throws him back on painting. Seeing in art a possible compensation for his physical deformity, his parents encourage him.**

1878 Paris World's Fair. Duret publishes " Les Peintres impressionnistes."

1879 Death of Daumier. Odilon Redon publishes an album of lithographs entitled " Dans le rêve."

1880 **His first teacher is René Princeteau, a painter of military and equestrian scenes, then he patterns his work after Lewis Brown. His first pictures show brilliant craftsmanship, virtuosity in drawing and a taste for " modern " subjects.**

1881 Birth of Picasso.

1882 **Lautrec decides to overhaul his art training from the very beginning, and after passing his " baccalaureate " at Toulouse in 1881, he enrolls in Bonnat's studio in 1882, then in Cormon's.**

1883 Death of Manet.

1884 **Influenced by Forain, parodies Puvis de Chavannes, discovers and admires the art of Manet, Berthe Morisot and Degas.**

1884 Founding of the Salon des Indépendants by Seurat, Signac, Cross and Redon, and of La Revue Indépendante (edited by Félix Fénéon). Manet Memorial Exhibition at the Ecole des Beaux-Arts. Gauguin leaves for Copenhagen.

1885 Pissarro meets Theo Van Gogh, then Signac and Seurat; adopts Pointillism in 1886. Van Gogh at Nuenen.

1886 At Cormon's studio Lautrec meets Van Gogh, who has just come to Paris. He rents a studio at the corner of the Rue Tourlaque and the Rue Caulaincourt in the heart of Montmartre, whose intense night-life supplies him with his favorite subjects. He frequents the Cirque Fernando, Bruant's famous Cabaret Artistique, Le Mirliton and Le Moulin de la Galette. Meets Pissarro, Degas, Gauguin and Seurat.

1886 Eighth and last Group Exhibition of the Impressionists. Degas exhibits a series of ten pastels of nude women. Revelation of the Douanier Rousseau at the Salon des Indépendants. Gauguin's first stay at Pont-Aven in Brittany. Rimbaud publishes his " Illuminations."

1887 Van Gogh meets Emile Bernard. Gauguin goes to Panama and Martinique. Mallarmé publishes his " Poésies complètes."

1888 Bonnard, Vuillard, Maurice Denis, Ranson and Sérusier meet at the Académie Julian. James Ensor paints his large-scale work : " The Entrance of Christ into Brussels." Acting on Lautrec's advice, Van Gogh leaves for Arles, where Gauguin joins him, with tragic results. Gauguin's first one-man show at Boussod and Valadon's. Gauguin's second stay at Pont-Aven with Emile Bernard; beginnings of Cloisonnism and Synthesism. Cézanne makes a long stay in Paris.

1889 Lautrec exhibits for the first time at the Salon des Indépendants with "Au bal du Moulin de la Galette." He paints a number of portraits in the garden of Le père Forest.

1889 Paris World's Fair. Construction of the Eiffel Tower. Verlaine publishes " Parallèlement." Gauguin's third stay in Brittany; paints " Le Christ jaune." Van Gogh enters the Saint-Rémy Asylum, near Arles.

1890 Munch's first stay in Paris; sees pictures by Pissarro, Seurat, Lautrec. Death of Van Gogh.

1891 Drawing inspiration from La Goulue's dance, Lautrec designs his first poster for the Moulin Rouge, using a new elliptical technique which soon appears in his painting.

1891 Van Gogh Retrospective Exhibition at the Indépendants, where Bonnard now exhibits for the first time. Death of Seurat. Gauguin leaves for Tahiti. The Natanson brothers launch " La Revue Blanche." Gatherings of Symbolist poets at the Café Voltaire (Place de l'Odéon). Aurier's Manifesto of Symbolist painting. First exhibition of the Nabis.

1892 Lautrec paints many pictures of Jane Avril and the dancing girls at the Moulin Rouge. First lithographs. Does posters for Le Divan japonais and Les Ambassadeurs, and paints a series of scenes from the "maisons closes" in the Rue d'Amboise.

1892 Seurat Retrospective Exhibition at " La Revue Blanche." Matisse arrives in Paris and enrolls at the Académie Julian.

1893 On Joyant's initiative, Lautrec exhibits with Charles Maurin at the Goupil Gallery, showing a number of pictures devoted to Montmartre life; Degas visits the exhibition and approves.

1893 Degas exhibits pastel landscapes at Durand-Ruel's. Opening of the Vollard Gallery. Matisse and Rouault meet in Gustave Moreau's studio. First exhibition of the Munich Secession.

1894 Lithographs on theatrical subjects ; first album of lithographs of Yvette Guilbert. His studies of the "maisons closes" culminate in a large composition : " Au Salon de la rue des Moulins." Visits Brussels.

1894 Caillebotte bequest to the Musée du Luxembourg.

1895 New series of scenes from the theater and music-hall: Marcelle Lender in Chilpéric, May Belfort, the clowness Cha-U-Kao. Decorates La Goulue's Booth at the Foire du Trône. Goes to London where he paints a portrait of Oscar Wilde and visits Whistler. Back in Paris, Lautrec is initiated into the sporting world by Tristan Bernard.

1895 First public motion-picture shows given by the Lumière brothers. At the Salon, Tiffany exhibits stained-glass windows after designs by Vuillard, Lautrec, Bonnard, Sérusier, Vallotton. Vollard publishes " Quelques aspects de la vie de Paris." Gauguin's second auction-sale at the Hôtel Drouot; he leaves for Tahiti for the second time. Publication of Rimbaud's " Poésies complètes," with a preface by Verlaine.

1896 Lautrec takes part in the first exhibition of " La Libre Esthé- tique " group at Brussels. In Holland with Maxime Dethomas, Spain and Portugal with Maurice Guibert ; discovers El Greco. Publishes a set of lithographs called " Elles. "

1896 Bonnard's first one-man show at Durand-Ruel's. Matisse's first appearance at the Salon de la Nationale. Death of Verlaine. Marcel Proust publishes " Les Plaisirs et les Jours."

1897 Lautrec moves from the Rue Tourlaque to a new studio in the Avenue Frochot. Gives up poster painting and concentrates on lithography, both in black-and-white and in colors. Frequent stays at Villeneuve-sur-Yonne with his friends the Natansons.

1897 " La Revue Blanche " publishes Gauguin's manuscript " Noa-Noa," while in Tahiti Gauguin paints his vast composition " Whence come we ? What are we ? Whither go we ? " Munch stays in Paris, doing lithographs and woodcuts.

1898 Goes to London during his exhibition at the Goupil Gallery. Health now badly shaken by night-life and heavy drinking.

1898 Mellerio publishes " La Lithographie originale en couleurs." Bonnard illustrates P. Nansen's " Marie." Death of Mallarmé.

1899 Illustrates Jules Renard's " Histoires naturelles." Lautrec is confined from February to May in the Saint-James clinic at Neuilly where attempts are made to break him of his drinking habits; it is here that he paints from memory the fine series " Le Cirque." Released as a result of a press campaign by his friends, he breaks his stays in Paris with trips to Bordeaux and Le Havre. In 1900 he paints pictures inspired by the opera " Messalina " at the Bordeaux opera house.

1899 Group Exhibition of the Nabis at Durand-Ruel's in homage to Odilon Redon. Matisse, Derain, Jean Puy and Laprade meet at the Académie Carrière. Signac publishes " D'Eugène Delacroix au Néo-Impressionnisme." Death of Sisley.

1900 Paris World's Fair. Seurat Retrospective Exhibition organized at " La Revue Blanche " by Félix Fénéon. Picasso's first stay in Paris.

1901 Lautrec's health deteriorates rapidly. Foreseeing the end, he asks to be taken to his mother and dies at the Château de Malromé on September 9, aged 37. His mother collected all the works in his studio and presented them to the town of Albi; they are housed in the Toulouse-Lautrec Museum, inaugurated on July 30, 1922, in the episcopal palace of La Berbie.

This summary has been drawn from the documentary material compiled by Mr Jean Leymarie for The History of Modern Painting *(Skira, 1949-1950).*

" What he is aiming at is to distill from the fashions of the day their poetic content ; to elicit the eternal from the ephemeral."

IN WRITING thus Baudelaire had Constantin Guys in mind, but to whom would these words apply more aptly than to Lautrec ? None saw better than he the elements of permanence in the ever-rolling stream of Time, and what he sought for in the theaters, circuses and dance-halls of Paris, in the streets, or behind the shutters of bawdyhouses, was the moment when human nature drops its mask and reveals its stark reality. Such sudden glimpses—" epiphanies "—come to a man almost accidentally, in the course of his life, his occupations, in casual encounters, incidents of visual experience. And the secret of Lautrec's art was its power of piercing through the surface of anecdotal, seeming-trivial, sometimes even ludicrous appearances, to the heart of the matter, the vital human core, and depicting unmasked human nature as it basically is.

His technical methods, his flair for the significant detail and his economy of means were the result of personal research alone and practical experience, and in the end he had trained his hand and eye to such perfection that they functioned almost automatically. When Lautrec made incessant variations on a set theme, sometimes spending weeks on end on a work that he effaced each evening and recommenced each morning, it was not, like Monet, to register the changing effects of light, or to build up a composition by successive stages. What he wanted was to express *everything* with but a few deft touches and to fine down his vision to essentials. (Fifty years later Matisse was to follow the same course.) With each sitting Lautrec gained an ever-deeper insight into his model; he expressed this in a form that, being a synthesis of previous discoveries, now came to him quite naturally. This last " style," the one he found most satisfying, may be perceived no less in his hastiest

9

sketches than in elaborately worked-out compositions. But what is known as " finish " was in no case his aim.

Lautrec never approached art from the aesthetic angle, and this is why he took no part in the controversies that raged between the various art movements at the close of the century. For he was at once older than his age and, in his eagerness to understand and register the diverse aspects of his epoch, younger than his contemporaries. He was in fact an artist of a different breed.

He was never actuated by any predilection for ugliness *per se*, and the distortions in his art are not a " transfer " of his own deformity. Nor is there any trace of repression, of the abnormal or pathological, in his work. He painted only that which came within the range of his personal experience, provided, after subjecting it to the acid test of his personal integrity, he judged it worthy of himself. In a word, he was a tireless observer of the world around him and trained his vision so effectively that he spares us no blemish on a model's face and achieves a truth to nature richer than nature herself. Which is what Tristan Bernard meant when he said that " by dint of being natural to the furthest conceivable limit, Lautrec attains the super-natural."

PHYSICAL APPEARANCE

N<small>O REAL</small> self-portrait by Toulouse-Lautrec exists, except a youthful work: a fleeting glimpse of a face reflected in a mirror, with a far-away look and indeterminate outlines. Portraits made in after years by his friends, Javal (1883), Anquetin (1889) and Adolphe Albert (1897), by Vuillard (1898) in the Natansons' home at Villeneuve-sur-Yonne, and by Maxime Dethomas (1898) at Granville, are more revealing. Harshest of all are the little effigies of himself that Lautrec made, doodling-wise, on restaurant tablecloths, or like pictographic signatures in the corners of sketches; in these he brought out frankly, if with a brevity confessing his reluctance, his physical deformity and the almost equal ugliness of his face.

Some photographs confirm this touching self-revelation. Oddly enough Lautrec liked donning fancy dress for dances in friends' houses and artists' balls, and he faced the camera as imperturbably when dressed up as a geisha as when wearing smart check trousers and a sporting overcoat skillfully tailored for his peculiar figure. We can gage his stature by several of his pictures which show him edging along between the tables at the Moulin Rouge, beside his constant companion (and cousin) Gabriel Tapié de Céleyran; Lautrec's head comes barely level with his cousin's chest.

Familiarity and the stoic acceptance of his lot to which these pictures testify have endeared to us that grotesque figure. A normally developed torso rises above two stunted, twisted legs. The head is covered with a mop of bristly hair carefully plastered down, and we see a short beard, straggly mustache, big nose and those puffy lips through which so often flowed a stream of broken phrases highly difficult to catch. Only the eyes were a redeeming feature; dark, lustrous eyes glowing behind the pince-nez.

Lautrec had a trick of stressing certain syllables, rolling his R's and sprinkling his talk with odd words charged with private meanings, the key to which only his friends possessed. Such were the words " Fontanges " (the name of Louis XIV's elegant mistress) and " *roupie* " (argot for a drop at the end of the nose), the former applied to things he found pleasant to see and the latter to those that disgusted him. Other pet words were " approach-tactics " and " technique " applied to sentimental occasions such as the progress of a love affair.

He had great difficulty in walking and always leant on a small stick (the " boot-hook " as he called it) which he took with him everywhere. But his activity was prodigious, he was always on the move and forced his cronies to accompany him wherever a sudden fancy prompted him to go. And he never lacked an escort of devoted friends, tamed to humor his caprices. In his *Memoirs* Thadée Natanson has much to tell us of those interminable nocturnal jaunts in which Lautrec kept postponing the moment of return, and the terrible depression that came over him at daybreak, when he had to face up to himself and drab reality.

His body had let him down, but he disciplined it as best he could and proved that, but for ill luck, he might have lived up to the traditions of a French family famed for its prowess on the hunting-field and the race-course. He was a fine swimmer and exercised his arm muscles on a " rowing machine " installed in his studio. He also went in for sailing and one of his greatest delights was navigating a yacht in the Bay of Arcachon, squatting on the deck, lashed by the sea-wind. Jules Renard neatly defined the impression of massive strength given by the upper half of Lautrec's body when he described the painter as " a tiny little blacksmith wearing pince-nez. "

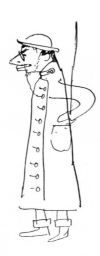

FAMILY BACKGROUND

Henri de Toulouse-Lautrec was born on November 24, 1864, at Albi, in the ancient Hôtel du Bosc, an austere private house in the Rue de l'Ecole Mage (now Rue Henri de Toulouse-Lautrec). His father, Count Alphonse de Toulouse-Lautrec-Monfa, had married his cousin-german, Adèle Tapié de Céleyran; the painter's two grandmothers were sisters, Gabrielle and Louise d'Imbert du Bosc.

Though its connection with the Counts of Toulouse, defenders of the persecuted Albigenses, is somewhat uncertain, the Toulouse-Lautrec family is a very ancient one, going back to Antoine, Viscount of Toulouse, Lautrec, Monfa, Saint-Germier and other places, who made his Will in 1527. The painter's childhood and early youth were spent in the various residences of his mother's family; at Albi, in the Château du Bosc (Aveyron Department), at the Château de Céleyran (Aude) and finally the Château de Malromé (Gironde), acquired in 1883.

Until his death, fortified with the rites of the Church, at Malromé, Lautrec lived in a family atmosphere, but this did not afflict or hamper him at all; he always made light of conventions and snapped his fingers at taboos. That great sportsman, his father, too, was nothing if not original and, while some of his eccentricities may seem to us a little futile, he certainly cut an impressive figure.

Count Alphonse had the true sportsman's code of honor and feeling for fair play. Joyant tells us that when out hunting he would stop the hunt, if English hounds, which did not give tongue in the French manner and warn the quarry, were employed. The last great falconer in France, he regarded the use of a gun as a sign of decadence. He collected exotic weapons and often clad himself in a Kirghiz coat-of-mail. Lautrec made many pictures of his father on horseback in the costume of the Indian Chief in *The Last of the Mohicans,* or dressed up as a Circassian with his favorite falcon on his wrist, or driving a spirited team of thoroughbreds, his beard and Inverness cape streaming in the wind.

COUNT ALPHONSE DE TOULOUSE-LAUTREC DRIVING HIS FOUR-IN-HAND AT NICE, 1881. 16⅞×20½") ON CANVAS. MUSÉE DU PETIT PALAIS, PARIS.

This country gentleman, whose eccentricities were a byword in the Paris clubs and at race-meetings, was a friend of Forain and the sporting painters Princeteau and Lewis Brown, and indeed was far from being a mere " Philistine." On a manual of falconry that he gave his son for his twelfth birthday he wrote: " *Remember, my son, that life in the open air and open country is the only healthy life. Every creature deprived of liberty soon degenerates and dies. This little book on falconry will teach you to enjoy the great open spaces and if one day things go badly with you, horses first of all, then dogs and falcons, will prove faithful friends and help you to forget your troubles.*" A letter that twenty-three years later Lautrec sent his father, asking him to obtain his release from a sanatorium where he was undergoing treatment for alcoholism, echoes his father's words. " *I am shut up, and everything that's shut up dies.*" Lautrec had no illusions about his father; he saw in him a sometimes exasperating ally who could be counted on to understand, if not his art, his way of living.

To his mother he looked not only for understanding but for love, and she was perhaps the only person in the world whose pity he accepted. She was a gentle, resigned woman, neglected by her husband and unhappy in her children: Henri, so delicate as a boy and crippled by an accident when in his teens, and Richard who died in babyhood. Whereas her brother Amédée (who married her husband's sister) was blessed with a family of fourteen, one of them being Gabriel Tapié de Céleyran. A kindly, capable woman, she successfully managed the family estate single-handed and saw to it that all were comfortably provided for. Practically her whole life was devoted to her son Henri; wherever he went she accompanied him, but kept discreetly in the background. And on the threshold of his mother's home, that sure place of refuge where Henri went almost daily, to eat, sleep or recover from his fits of depression, the mystery of his " double life " begins. . .

COUNTESS DE TOULOUSE-LAUTREC BREAKFASTING AT MALROMÉ, 1883.
(36¼ × 31½″) ON CANVAS. MUSÉE D'ALBI.

Lautrec took infinite pains over the big portraits he made of his mother. He always showed her in pensive attitudes, with downcast eyes, her face bathed in discreetly subdued light.

RIDER AND LED HORSE, 1882. (6½×9¼″) ON WOOD.
MUSÉE D'ALBI.

YOUTH AND EARLY TRAINING

THERE was nothing in the least unusual about Henri de Toulouse-Lautrec's childhood. He was brought up amongst a host of cousins, boys and girls, at Le Bosc and Céleyran, and studied at home, learning the rudiments of Latin and Greek from local priests. And in the sheltered, easy-going atmosphere of his home life he was able to develop freely, on his own lines.

In 1873 the family settled at Paris, in the Hotel Pérey, Cité du Retiro. Henri enrolled in the 1st (lowest) Form at the Lycée Fontanes (now the Lycée Condorcet). When in the 2nd Form he carried off all the prizes in French and Latin. Amongst his schoolmates were his cousin Louis Pascal and also Maurice Joyant, who was destined to be his lifelong friend. But his health, always delicate, deteriorated and he soon was heading for a nervous breakdown, with the result that he had to leave school and study with private tutors, under the supervision of his mother, who carried maternal devotion to the point of learning Latin and English so as to help him in his studies.

Henri showed a talent for drawing and exceptional powers of observation at a very early age. The margins of his exercise-books (which have been preserved) are full of little sketches: caricatures of his parents, teachers, schoolmates, and also purely imaginary forms, graphic images of ideas that sometimes amounted to obsessions. For already he had formed a habit of harking back to the same themes again and again, making variations on them and showing them under all their aspects. He was especially fond of drawing domestic animals, particularly horses, and in sketching them he abandoned the lively, almost slapdash method of his caricatures and developed in successive versions of the same theme a remarkable, steadily increasing sureness and accuracy of line.

Then, when he was only fourteen, he had the first of the seemingly trivial, but in fact momentous, accidents whose consequences were to darken all his future life. On May 30, 1878, when he was with his mother and grandmother in the drawing-room of their place at Albi, he slipped on the polished floor and broke his left thigh. It was put in plaster and he was sent to " do a cure " at Barèges and also at Amélie-les-Bains. In August 1879, when out walking with his mother in the neighborhood of Barèges, he stumbled into a ditch and broke his right thigh. Owing to what was probably a congenital deficiency in the osseous structure, the bones never joined up properly, with the result that though he had a normal stature from the waist up, his legs stopped growing and remained disproportionately short throughout the remainder of his life.

He faced this disaster with courage, and even good humor. During the trying period of convalescence he sent amusing letters and " travelogues " to his friends and cousins. The best known of these, quaintly named *Le Cahier de Zigzags*, was sent from Nice (in 1881) to his cousin Madeleine Tapié. There is nothing forced in the cheerful tone of the letters, and the self-control they reveal is nothing short of heroic, especially when we remember their writer's age. Not only does Lautrec refrain from any self-pity, but he seems bent on discouraging others from condoling with him. Rather, he tends to stress the comic aspects of his infirmity, so as to make it ludicrous— and thus, perhaps, innocuous. During this period he did some witty illustrations for a story named (after an old horse) *Cocotte*, written in 1880 by Etienne Devismes, with whom he had struck up a friendship at Barèges.

Meanwhile a fresh, all-absorbing interest was gradually giving a new direction to Lautrec's life; he was beginning to paint. And his painting served as a compensation, for he found that with his brush he could impart a colorful vitality to scenes in which he was now forbidden to play an active part. We may be sure that it was due to more than mere caprice that so many dashing horsemen and showy four-in-hands figured amongst his early efforts in this field. The stages of his development as an artist coincide exactly with those of his illnesses. His first paintings date to the end of 1878 or the beginning of 1879. From the start we see the influence of René Princeteau; it is particularly obvious in his *Memory of Chantilly* which shows the Lautrec family driving back from the races in a victoria.

The exhibition at Albi in 1952, in which Lautrec's juvenile productions (recollections of the Army Maneuvers at Le Bosc in 1879, artillerymen, his first paintings of four-in-hands and so forth) were shown alongside works by Princeteau, hunting and steeplechasing scenes, made this debt apparent. We have here an influence that lasted for two or three years and, in some respects, left a permanent mark on Lautrec's art. Princeteau, who hailed from Bordeaux, was a personal friend of the Comte de Toulouse-Lautrec whom he often painted as a steeplechase-rider. Perhaps the fact that he was a deaf-mute made a bond of sympathy between him and his crippled pupil. Anyhow, he was quick to realize the boy's gifts and gave him a thorough grounding in the technique of a form of art that, unadventurous though it was, still suited the tastes of the young beginner, conditioned as these were by his surroundings. In some unpublished letters Princeteau praises the liveliness and adroitness of young Lautrec's brushwork and calls him humorously but affectionately " a regular little ape." In fact his pupil's mimetic gift was such that he could reproduce almost effortlessly what in Princeteau's case was due to lifelong study. (Later on, too, Lautrec used to amuse himself by painting " in the manner of " his most eminent contemporaries.)

Lautrec borrowed from Princeteau his themes and his technical devices for presenting human figures or horses under aspects displaying their forms and poise to best effect. Notably he learnt from him a rather special procedure enabling him to render, with dainty brushstrokes spreading fanwise, the subtle effects of light playing on costumes or horses' coats in forest interiors. This was only remotely connected with the breaking-up of colors practiced by the Impressionists, but their theories were " in the air," and the worthy Princeteau tried in his own way to supersede the dry, precise linework of the traditionalist animal-painter and to convey the vibrancy of moving forms. Under Lautrec's brush this supple, sketch-like technique acquired new life; always fond of painting in the open, he bathed his models in limpid air and reversed the relations between light and dark obtaining in most of the painting of the day. Instead of placing bright passages on somber grounds, he posed his figures against the light, and by using a luminous background brought outlines into prominence and enhanced the brightness of the colors.

The paintings he made early in 1880 at Nice are in this vein and show steady progress in the expression of rhythm and movement. Many are mere sketches, but are none the less effective. The subjects are women on horseback accompanied by grooms or greyhounds, and elegant ladies driving showy turn-outs at the gallop. *The Black Countess* (so called simply because her face is seen in shadow against a backcloth of sea, sky and palmtrees) is typical. Here Lautrec had in mind the illustrations in *La Vie Parisienne* and the works, rather like fashion plates, of John Lewis Brown, in which great care is given to rendering figures and gestures, and little to the execution of details.

In these small pictures—frankly amazing when we remember their maker's youth—Lautrec achieved a skillful balance between poetic inspiration and factual truth. But it is interesting to see how rapidly he exhausted the possibilities of subjects which sufficed painters like Princeteau and Brown for a whole life's work. Lautrec's art never hardened into a system—which is why he so quickly outdistanced his teachers. In summer 1880 he made his first landscape views, one of Albi, but for the most

A PRIEST (DETAIL), 1881. ON CANVAS. MUSÉE D'ALBI.　　▶

Lautrec, who had a wonderful knack of imitation, adopted Princeteau's technique of rendering the play of light on colored surfaces by means of little brushstrokes spreading fanwise. He employed this technique not only in his many pictures of horses (this subject, too, he took from Princeteau) but also in his early portraits. Here he has mottled the priest's florid face with vivid patches of pure red, employing a sort of color-expressionism of his own invention.

part of Céleyran, and it is interesting to note in these his use of light, wavy, adroitly placed brushstrokes for rendering scenes of the countryside. Later in the year he sought to deepen his understanding of nature and to individualize not only persons but the domestic animals at Le Bosc, for example a white horse, named " Gazelle," of which he made what may be called quite justly half-length portraits. Also he made careful studies of human models, members of the Toulouse-Lautrec household to begin with: his father, mother, cousins, family friends, farmers and old retainers.

In 1881, after spending the spring in Paris, he sat for his baccalaureate, but failed; however he was successful in October at Toulouse. This was his last concession to the family views on education; he had now decided to devote himself exclusively to painting. Here Princeteau's friendly aid stood him in good stead and overcame his parents' scruples. Lautrec returned to Paris in March 1882 and started work in the studio of his old friend and teacher at 233 Faubourg Saint-Honoré, an artist center where Lewis Brown, too, was living and where he met Forain. But he learnt little from these artists and soon struck out on his own lines. Only a year before, he was still employing Princeteau's small, scattered touches, as in that amazing *Priest* with his mottled face on a ground of almost the same color, a work whose vigor and assured craftsmanship are remarkable. But by the summer of 1882 a vast change had come over his art. Though the subjects seem to belong to the rustic genre then favored by the " official " school of painting (Jules Breton, Léon Lhermitte and Bastien-Lepage), his handling of them was as far removed from naturalism as from the conventional scenes of peasant life. His light, glaucous color —pale greens framed in clean-cut, almost over-precise outlines— reminds us of Whistlerian " harmonies," while the small criss-cross touches, no longer tentative and blurred but delicately

GUEULE DE BOIS OR THE DRINKER, 1889. (18½ × 21¾") WERTHEIM
COLLECTION, FOGG ART MUSEUM, CAMBRIDGE, MASS.

Suzanne Valadon posed for this picture, on which Lautrec set much
store. Two preparatory studies are in Albi Museum. A drawing inspired
by it appeared in *Le Courrier Français* (April 21, 1889). Van Gogh, a
pastel portrait of whom Lautrec had just finished, was present when this
picture was started and the influence of his technique is manifest. In a
letter to his brother (April, 1888) he inquires if Lautrec has finished his
picture. Here Lautrec's brushwork has an over-all homogeneity; the criss-
cross strokes are applied evenly and not as yet stepped up to "accents."

laid on—greys, mauves and white—recall Berthe Morisot, that is to say the species of Impressionism most acceptable to the *milieu* of society painters which Lautrec still frequented.

His tendency towards a sort of unavowed Impressionism took two forms. We find broad tracts of color and skillfully contrasted planes in that curious likeness of a friend, *Le Couteulx riding a Donkey* (1880, Albi Museum), and the portrait of his mother seated in the garden, her face half hidden by a blue cloche hat, against a background of sunlit leafage. On the other hand, in the portraits of Routy (1882, Basel and Albi Museums) and the big picture (1883, Albi) of his mother breakfasting at the Château de Malromé, he employs a quite different technique. These pictures show a notable advance on their predecessors and already point the way to Lautrec's " cold " painting. Pale colors and adroit juxtapositions of white passages give emphasis to the precision and vivacity of the calligraphy, which is implemented by delicate hatchings in pure color. Notable is the loving care the painter has expended on depicting his mother's half-shut eyes; while the prominence of the foreground, in which the hands are perceptibly enlarged and the coffee-cup is broadly mirrored in the polished table, foreshadows the compositional schemes we find in the works of his maturity.

PARIS, ART SCHOOLS, MONTMARTRE

Now came a break in Lautrec's evolution. At the instance of his family, most probably, but also perhaps out of curiosity and a sense of duty, he decided to see what could be learnt from the recognized art schools. For this he had to retrace his steps and, starting off again from the beginning, try to forget the knowledge he had acquired, in (it must be admitted) a haphazard way, guided chiefly by his instinct and emotions. Sponsored by a friend, the painter Henri Rachou, who also hailed from Albi and was studying under Bonnat, and introduced by Princeteau, Lautrec enrolled at the end of 1882 in Bonnat's school. Bonnat was then regarded as the leading exponent of the " official " type of portrait.

This venture lasted only a few months. Though extraordinarily mature for his age, Lautrec gave an impression of extreme youth, and this may account for the teacher's complete failure to realize that his new pupil had the makings of a genius. In any case Bonnat mistrusted juvenile originality and kept his class busy turning out academic nudes. Thus not only did Lautrec's drawing strike him as " simply atrocious," but he saw positively dangerous tendencies in Lautrec's work; tendencies which, if given their head, might well spell the ruin of all French art. (It was he who in 1903 caused the Luxembourg Museum to turn down the bequest of the portrait of M. Delaporte, and when in 1920 the portrait of Paul Leclercq was accepted by the National Museum, he sighed dolefully: " A fine mess we're making of the Louvre !") Lautrec, however, always stood up for Bonnat's artistic integrity and competence when, as often happened, his old teacher came under fire.

At the studio Lautrec did his utmost to please his master and, keeping his natural inclinations well in hand, plodded away conscientiously at distasteful tasks. But these meritorious efforts were lost on Bonnat, though, on the other hand, he was popular with his fellow-students, despite the odd figure he cut amongst them with his queer physical appearance and ultra-dandified attire. When in 1883 Bonnat's school closed, the group moved over to Cormon's in the Avenue de Clichy, and Lautrec worked there more or less steadily until 1885.

Here the atmosphere was very different. Cormon was an amiable, absent-minded artist who had never grown out of the art-student's fondness for practical jokes. Appreciative of his teacher's eccentricities, Lautrec got on with him extremely well. In his unpublished *Memoirs* the Toulouse painter François Gauzi tells of his amazement when, after studying in the severely academic *milieu* of the School of Fine Arts at Toulouse, he came to Cormon's studio and found Lautrec showing Cormon outrageously bold productions, defending his procedures vigorously—and, more surprising still, the master examining them with an indulgent eye. It was now that Lautrec made his clever parody of Puvis de Chavannes' *Sacred Wood* (exhibited in the 1884 Salon), which he transformed into a vulgar scene of " indecent assault " ! Indeed he never lost a taste for burlesques of grave and ancient themes and delighted in the light opera of the day in which the comic possibilities of this vein were exploited to the full.

Meanwhile in various studios he struck up friendships with his compatriots Rachou and Gauzi, with Emile Bernard the friend and rival of Gauguin who claimed to have invented " Cloisonnism," and with Louis Anquetin, an artist of marked originality. Other less known painters, amongst them Adolphe Albert the etcher (who introduced him to the " Indépendants " group), Joseph Albert and Grenier, whose wife had been Degas' model, now became his friends, and their devotion never failed him.

It was doubtless due to Bonnat's influence that Lautrec now and then reverted to a soberer, more somber style and achieved the smooth enamel finish we find in the work he did from models such as the red-haired " Carmen " (of whom he made many studies) and that other young person who figures in *The Washerwoman* (Mme Dortu's Collection) and other works. Meanwhile, however, he did not abandon his earlier technique; indeed we see him using it with more confidence and freedom in other portraits—e.g. those of Juliette Pascal and Suzanne Valadon (Carlsberg Glyptotek, Copenhagen)—and the curious decorations he painted in the winter of 1885 on the walls and doors of the Ancelin Inn at Villiers-sur-Morin. One of the four items in this picture sequence was *The Ballet* (Art Institute, Chicago) showing a bevy of dancers illuminated by unseen footlights and in the foreground the huge hands of a conductor; another, *The Gallery*, showing a row of spectators with grotesque heads reminiscent of Goya and Daumier.

Thus in his early twenties Lautrec had found himself, and felt sure he had chosen his vocation rightly. Not that he had any superiority complex; on the contrary, he was always ready to appreciate the works of others, wax enthusiastic over them and praise them generously, and he rarely had a hard word for a brother artist. But his modesty led him to regard the art of his great contemporaries, whom he was soon to equal, as beyond his range; such heights were not for him. His first idol was Degas, next came Renoir whose works he never tired of contemplating, marveling at the enamel-like luster of the colors. But, despite Degas' often quoted remark, " Well, Lautrec, I can see you're one of our trade!" it is doubtful if these artists saw in him much more than a brilliant amateur. Forain never took him seriously; but we must remember that Lautrec, too, much as he admired Forain's concise, spirited drawing, never considered him a great painter.

It was in Cormon's studio that Lautrec met Van Gogh, his senior by ten years, and he was vastly impressed by his personality, his deep sincerity, his wholehearted devotion to his art, his spiritual fervor—and his tragic lot. Full of generous enthusiasm and an ardent champion of Van Gogh during his lifetime, he venerated his memory, and at a banquet of the "XX" group at Brussels challenged Henri de Groux, who had spoken disparagingly of the dead painter, to a duel. He was much interested in Van Gogh's experiments during the period when, newly come to Paris, he was toying with Divisionism and, without adopting the systematized procedures of the Neo-Impressionists, finding ways of his own for incorporating pure color in his brushstrokes, thus strengthening their texture. For Lautrec much preferred practical demonstrations to theories; hence his vast respect for Van Gogh and his habit of twitting Gauguin for his dogmatism. In Van Gogh's art he found both a justification of his youthful ventures and an encouragement to press them further. From now on he knew that the life of a work of art stems not from any static compromise but from those vital rhythms which the painter expresses in his style and weaves into his arabesques.

In 1885 Lautrec decided to cut adrift from his family and devote his life to art exclusively. After leaving the Hotel Pérey, he began by lodging with his friends the Greniers at 19 bis Rue Fontaine (Degas' studio was at the back of the courtyard). Meanwhile he worked in Rachou's studio, 22 Rue Ganneron, then in Gauzi's, 7 Rue Tourlaque. Suzanne Valadon was living in the same house; Lautrec liked her work and used her as a model. In 1887 he moved into the house of Dr Bourges, in the Rue Fontaine, and stayed on there until his friend's marriage in 1893, when he returned to his mother's home in the Rue de Douai. For his work he rented a studio at 27 Rue Caulaincourt, which he occupied until 1897.

AT THE CIRQUE FERNANDO: CIRCUS RIDER, 1888. (39¼×78½″)
ON CANVAS. JOSEPH WINTERBOTHAM COLLECTION. BY COURTESY OF THE ART
INSTITUTE OF CHICAGO.

In view of its date, this is one of the landmarks in Lautrec's career. At
the time when he still was posing his models in almost classical attitudes,
and painting dancers at rest, he ventured here into a new field, showing
each figure in a moment of tense action, and adjusting the entire composition to the distortions given the figure in the foreground (the famous
" M. Loyal ") and the almost sculptural mass formed by the horse and
its rider. The onlookers on the rows of seats are deftly indicated by a
procedure foreshadowing the composition of *The Five Shirtfronts*, another
circus scene painted three years later. From his earliest days Lautrec
was a devotee of the circus; he often visited the Cirque Fernando (already
depicted by Degas, Renoir and Seurat), the Nouveau Cirque and the
equestrian show run by that famous riding-master Molier. Years later
in the *Circus* series, made in 1899 in a sanatorium, he evoked with a quite
amazing brio his memories of these scenes.

The Dihaus, a musical family related to his, and great friends of Degas, lived nearby. Désiré was a bassoonist in the Opera orchestra and a song-composer, his sister (painted by Degas in 1868) a pianist. In this humble home hung Degas' famous picture *The Orchestra at the Opera* (c. 1868) and Lautrec often came to gaze at it with pious admiration. Lautrec, too, painted his friends' portraits, and also designed covers for Désiré's songs. In the same street was the Goupil print-shop, the management of which Joyant had now taken over from Theo Van Gogh, and Lautrec and his former schoolmate became inseparable, Joyant doing for his friend what Theo had done for Van Gogh, showing constant interest in his work and trying to find a public for it. It was Joyant who wrote the best biography of his friend after his death and did most to ensure his lasting fame.

Montmartre had not yet become the Parisians' playground, and was merely a rather ill-famed outlying district of the city. Dotted with shacks and little gardens, the hill had an almost countryfied air. Rue Tourlaque was on the outskirts of this unbuilt area, just beyond the Montmartre cemetery. Where the Gaumont picture-house now stands were the straggling gardens of a well-to-do Parisian, known as " Père Forest," whose hobby was archery; he had set up an archery range and refreshment bar in his grounds. Here Lautrec posed his models and made many portraits between 1888 and 1891.

MADEMOISELLE DIHAU AT THE PIANO, 1890. (26¾ × 19″) ON CARDBOARD. ▶
MUSÉE D'ALBI.

Lautrec had qualms about making this picture, which was to take its place beside the portrait of Mlle Dihau painted by Degas in 1868. The preparatory drawing, boldly blocked out in red on the cardboard, shows through the blue over-painting. Long, luminous brushstrokes stress the hands (Joyant tells us that Lautrec had an idea of making " portraits of hands "). According to Mr Gerstle Mack, Van Gogh had this picture in mind in his *Mademoiselle Gachet at the Piano*.

EDGAR DEGAS (1834-1917). THE ORCHESTRA AT THE PARIS OPERA, C. 1868.
(20¾×17⅝") ON CANVAS. LOUVRE, PARIS.

He was soon a familiar figure in the district; he haunted its cafés, bars and dance-halls and used the street-walkers he met there as his models. In this little self-contained world on the periphery of Paris, which, while catering to the taste of the pleasure-seeker, was not yet making a business of it, and where everyone was free to amuse himself as he thought best, Lautrec felt happily at home.

In 1886 one of his favorite haunts was "Le Mirliton," a tavern kept by Bruant and immortalized by Courteline in *Messieurs les Ronds-de-Cuir*. Singer and chronicler of the Parisian underworld and its light-o'-loves, Bruant was a genius in his line. Lautrec did illustrations for his famous songs, *A Batignolles*, *A Belleville*, *A Saint-Lazare*, and drawings for a small magazine bearing the name of the tavern; also for *Le Courrier Français* and *Paris Illustré*. The exigencies of reproduction in this form led Lautrec gradually to simplify his drawing. In these works the whole composition hinges on a single line, sometimes interrupted but giving the over-all effect of a continuous, unbroken arabesque. On the walls of "Le Mirliton" he made a painting on the lines of those in the Ancelin Inn, *Le Quadrille de la Chaise Louis XIII*, in which La Goulue makes her first appearance in his art; a monochrome composition built up with small, excited brushstrokes. Under the influence of Bruant he also did some drawings with a social reference, such as *The Last Farewell*, showing a rough-looking workman doffing his hat to a passing hearse. One of the models he used

EDGAR DEGAS. THE ORCHESTRA AT THE PARIS OPERA.

In the foreground is Désiré Dihau the bassoonist. Lautrec often came to see this picture, the Dihaus' most treasured possession, "to say his prayers before it." He also brought friends to see it, sometimes in the small hours of the morning after a festive night. This lay-out, a narrow strip of illuminated stage and, outlined against it, the forms of musical instruments, was sometimes used by Lautrec; notably in his *Divan Japonais*.

for his pictures based on song themes (e.g. *A Montrouge*, 1888) was a particularly ugly woman known as " Rosa la Rouge."

In this phase—which, if not directly influenced by Bruant, reflects his attitude to life—Lautrec made a series of pictures whose titles were probably given by Bruant, as the painter rarely troubled to baptize the offspring of his brush. These names stress, perhaps unduly, the " social criticism " which Aristide Bruant chose to read into them: *Gueule de bois* (1889), *En Meublé* (1890), *A la mie* (1891), *Alfred la Guigne* (1894). This was the only time when Lautrec in posing his models— Suzanne Valadon in *Gueule de bois*, Maurice Guibert as the drunkard in *A la mie*—forced them to adopt attitudes that ran counter to their personalities in normal life. Ordinarily he studied the psychology of his sitters with such acuteness that even in mere practice studies he showed them as individuals with temperaments of their own.

Among Lautrec's most character-revealing portraits, those in which he makes us feel most clearly his deep understanding of human nature—whether viewed from an ironic or an amiable angle—are those he painted with unflagging zest in the years 1888-1891. The models were for the most part women of no particular standing and in many cases are known to us only by their first names; Hélène V. and Marie Charlet (dressed as a dancer) with whom he had protracted love-affairs, Augusta, Gabrielle, the police-sergeant's daughter, deaf Bertha, Casque d'Or the street-walker, Justine Dieuhl, and Honorine P., " the woman with the glove."

Rather stiffly posed to begin with, and telling out against the neutral background of a studio, these almost hieratic figures gradually won through to freedom and a grandeur of their own, vibrant with the breath of life. Soon, however, Lautrec moved his figures from the studio into the open, the gardens of " Père Forest." Not that he was much interested

AUGUSTA, 1890. (24×15⅜″) ON CARDBOARD. FOGG ART
MUSEUM, CAMBRIDGE, MASS.

in the natural scene which served them as a background; indeed he treats this quite summarily, with only brief, perfunctory indications of leafage and so forth. Only on rare occasions—as in the portraits of his friends Henri and Désiré Dihau—does he take advantage of the setting and include tracts of complementary colors in the composition. He drew and painted at the same time, in series of light touches. Strongly diluted with turpentine, his colors are always pure (no Sienna figures on the palette now to be seen in Albi Museum), and so disposed as to avoid contrasts tending to " kill " the values. They were applied broadly and rapidly to the surface of the canvas or cardboard, sometimes letting the natural color of the mount show through.

Nor does he take account of the changes in the model's appearance caused by the variations of the light according to the time of day. On the contrary Lautrec constantly uses a cold, abstract, so to speak ideal light that does not play tricks with the model's features, but enables the painter to analyze the human face with almost scientific precision and to reveal its inmost secrets.

This, then, is the explanation of Lautrec's " cold light " (as Mac Orlan has named it). It was the result of a long study of daylight and, as we have suggested, a sublimation of it, and henceforth Lautrec always used this light both in open-air and studio painting. True, in his night-life scenes this light would have been inappropriate; footlights, for instance, by illuminating faces from below, cause deformations of the features, but Lautrec made this anomaly serve his turn, as a means of stressing facial expression. In any case it did not alter his general conception of painting as an art whence shadow should be banned as far as possible, the use of it being a confession of incompetence or of cowardice. In fact Lautrec always regarded painting as a victory over the indistinct.

WOMAN IN THE GARDEN OF M. FOREST, 1891. (24½ × 21½″)
MUSEUM OF ART, TOLEDO, OHIO.

Here, as in most of Lautrec's open-air work, the landscape element is
hastily sketched in. This use of colors diluted with turpentine for painting
on cardboard (whose greyish ground he here embodies in his color
scheme) was taken over by him from Raffaëlli.

LA GOULUE AND VALENTIN-LE-DÉSOSSÉ, 1890. (23⅞ × 19⅝″)
ON CARDBOARD. HAHNLOSER COLLECTION, WINTERTHUR.

AT THE MOULIN ROUGE

WHEN Lautrec brought off what had long been his ambi-
tion and tackled large-scale composition, the elements
he used were those he had already wholly mastered, as described above. Indeed in his first depictions of the big Montmartre dance-halls the women have almost the same faces as
those of the girls of easy virtue whose portraits he had painted
in Forest's gardens.

His first hunting-ground was the Elysée-Montmartre
dance-hall where La Goulue made her début and where a
male embodiment of Mrs Grundy known as " Père la Pudeur "
was delegated by the powers-that-be to see to it that the bounds
of decency were not overstepped. Lautrec began by trying to
reproduce the general movement of the crowd and, to secure
this effect, he slashed the picture surface with vivid brushstrokes which at once indicated individual features and linked
up the wildly gyrating dancers in an all-over rhythm. Indeed
when La Goulue and Valentin-le-Désossé make their first
appearance it is only by their ultra-extravagant contortions
that we distinguish them from the others.

Soon, however—and this synchronizes with the period
when he completely mastered portraiture—Lautrec turned to
compositions at once more significant and more detailed. His
new scene of action was the Moulin de la Galette, immortalized by Renoir in its palmy days, but which now had quite
changed its character, its habitués coming from much lower
social strata. The girls and oldish women who now frequented
it affected the costumes of the apache-haunted no-man's-land
on the outskirts of the city, and one saw a mixed crowd of
pimps and prostitutes, interspersed with girls of the working
class, gyrating in the thick, smoke-laden atmosphere of the

dance-hall. Lautrec included in these group scenes the individual type-figures to which he had given so much study
in the past. Thus in *Le Moulin de la Galette* (1889, Art Institute,
Chicago) we are shown, against a background of picturesque but
rather vaguely rendered dancers, the equine profile of Joseph
Albert and a group of young women including Jeanne Fontaine
(the *Girl with the Fur* in another work), her hair dressed in a
high yellow chignon.

For in these crowd compositions Lautrec had a habit of
inserting his friends, the familiar faces that always hovered
before his mind's eye. And, paradoxically enough, their
personalities gained in intensity by these contacts with the
crowd. Here we have yet another instance of his over-riding
interest in the individual personality.

The earliest pictures he made at the Moulin Rouge, then in
its heyday, are dominated by a single, all-pervasive rhythm,
that of the dance. But here the spirit of the dance is incarnated
in an almost brutally realistic form: in La Goulue. Lautrec
had had his eye on her from the start of her career, applying
his wonderful powers of observation to the study of her least
gestures. When in 1891 he was commissioned to make a new
poster for the Moulin Rouge, to replace the famous one by
Chéret, which had bedecked the walls of Paris with a colorful
bevy of sprightly, alluring young women, he made La Goulue

AT THE MOULIN ROUGE, LA GOULUE, 1891. (60½×46⅜″) CHARCOAL WITH ▶
COLOR WASH. MUSÉE D'ALBI.

A sketch for Lautrec's first poster. The dancer's form, all in billowing
curves and light frills, is skillfully contrasted with that of Valentin-
le-Désossé, all angles, clean-cut facets. His role is reduced to that of
a mere stage property placed there to stress his partner's ample charms.
Lautrec leads the observer's eye into the very center of the scene, between
the main subject and the marginal planes, thus inviting him to participate
in the life of that queer, faintly sinister world of the old Moulin Rouge,
among whose denizens were many celebrities of the day.

43

THE MOULIN ROUGE (DETAIL), 1890. BY COURTESY OF
MR HENRY P. MCILHENNY, PHILADELPHIA.

THE MOULIN ROUGE, 1890. (45 ¼ × 59″) ON CANVAS. BY COURTESY OF
MR HENRY P. MCILHENNY, PHILADELPHIA.

This picture, which was bought by the manager of the Moulin Rouge
and hung by him in the entrance of the music-hall, is laid out in three
distinct planes. In the background, amongst a group of spectators treated
caricaturally, we see Guibert, Sescau and Gauzi. In the middle distance
Lautrec—so as to render the impression produced by a dancing couple—
has painted on the floor a curious arabesque that is not a mere shadow
but a sort of after-image of the movements of the dancers. In front are
the usual promenaders, one of them intersected by the frame.

its leading figure. He depicted her in an attitude synthesizing the fantastic dance steps that were her speciality. A preliminary sketch (in Albi Museum) shows how he went about this. Flooded with light and holding the center of the composition, she stands out against a background of black forms, balanced in the foreground by her gaunt, gangling, almost sinister opposite number, Valentin-le-Désossé.

This lay-out is characteristic. Lautrec gives his central figures their full value by placing them at the salient point of a perspective vista built up by a system of ascending diagonals, setting the horizon line rather high in the composition. Here lies the difference between his lay-outs and those of his friend Bonnard who, in his *France-Champagne* poster (1889), used figures seen in *descending* perspective, as if floating in space.

Bonnard used to wonderful effect an undulating arabesque enabling him to dapple the entire picture surface with patches of subtle colors, giving it richness and variety. Densely patterned like some Eastern textiles, his work brilliantly implemented the possibilities of the lithograph, but was less suited for figuring on walls. Lautrec went about the poster in a different way. Above all he wished his line to lose nothing of its vigor when seen at a distance, and with this in mind he simplified and thickened it, filling out the spaces which it demarcated with vivid, juxtaposed colors.

Thus in his first posters we have as it were enlarged versions, in a form more accessible to the public, of all he had achieved after years of assiduous study, in the field of the picture proper. And, reciprocally, his painting was affected by these contacts with a public far wider than that which visited picture exhibitions (from 1889 on, Lautrec showed at the "Indépendants" and the Cercle Volney). Stripped down to essentials, it became bolder, freer, more direct in its appeal, while his line too gained a new incisiveness.

AT THE MOULIN ROUGE, 1892. (47¼×55″) ON CANVAS. BY COURTESY OF
THE ART INSTITUTE OF CHICAGO.
COLOR PHOTOGRAPH BY RICHARD J. BRITTAIN.

Here we see not the dancers but the public behind the barrier. Seated at a table are Sescau, Guibert and the poet Edouard Dujardin. In the background, her arms raised, La Goulue is settling her hair. Tapié de Céleyran is walking past and, with him, Lautrec himself, cutting a tiny figure beside his tall companion. In the foreground is a bizarre-looking woman (" Nelly C.") bathed in the full glare of lights situated outside the picture area, and oddly reminiscent of a green and yellow Chinese lantern.

We see this transformation at work in the big compositions of 1892 in which Lautrec, while keeping to themes provided by the Moulin Rouge and Parisian night-life, strengthened his effects by cutting out all merely anecdotal elements. Each of the performers in the Quadrille served him in turn as the focal point of a new variation, in which he stressed the dancer's personality to the utmost.

Pride of place is given La Goulue, who with her pinnacle of bright red hair, hawk nose, imperious mien and the fine carriage of her head and shoulders seems an incarnation of the innate nobility of certain women of the people who come of ancient stock. She was quite uneducated and probably stupid, but an instinctive urge led her to identify herself with her art, to *live* it totally, passionately. By dint of strenuous exercises she had made her limbs so supple that she could twist her body into the most incredible positions, and she had all the tricks of the floor dancer's art at her command. In her Lautrec found what he had always been seeking: the total integration

LA GOULUE ENTERING THE MOULIN ROUGE, 1892. $(31\frac{3}{8} \times 23\frac{1}{2}'')$ ▶
ON CARDBOARD. DR. AND MRS. DAVID M. LEVY COLLECTION, NEW YORK.

Planned and exploited by shrewd businessmen, the Moulin Rouge catered to a public of the upper classes, provincials and foreigners who were regaled with a colorful variety show and the possibility of sampling " low life " in a more or less luxurious setting. Lautrec began by illustrating its over-all atmosphere, but soon turned his attention to the individuals he met there, both artists and habitués. In that finely balanced and brilliantly executed composition, *La Goulue entering the Moulin Rouge*, we see her walking between her sister, a lump of a woman, and a pretty young dancer, shown side-face. At the Moulin Rouge Lautrec met some Englishmen who became his friends: Wilde, Charles Conder, Arthur Symons (who dedicated poems to Yvette Guilbert and Jane Avril), and Warrener, a Lincolnshire businessman. The preliminary sketch at Albi shows how Lautrec constructed his figures before transferring them to the large-scale works where they were to be included (in this case, with readjustments) in a complicated architectural arrangement of forms and colors.

THE ENGLISHMAN AT THE MOULIN ROUGE, 1892. (22¾ × 18⅞″)
ON CARDBOARD. MUSÉE D'ALBI.

THE ENGLISHMAN AT THE MOULIN ROUGE, 1892. (31¾ × 15″) ON CARDBOARD. ▶
A. M. DE GROOT COLLECTION, METROPOLITAN MUSEUM OF ART, NEW YORK.

of a human personality with its function. Contrasted with this plenitude of soft, voluptuous curves we see the brittle, angular form of Valentin-le-Désossé, all skin and bones, like a stage property put there to stress her ample charms.

As the months pass a sort of slowing down of the rhythms makes itself felt. It is now at the moment just before they fling themselves again into the Quadrille that Lautrec paints the dancers. One can see that they are tired, their limbs are aching. There are more queer characters about; tense, puffy-faced Lesbians prowl gloomily around tables at which haggard-eyed men are drinking. One feels that all these people, now they are no longer keyed up by the passionate excitement of the dance, are being gradually drained of their vitality, losing interest. . . But now Lautrec turned away towards more strongly molded faces, more stable characters.

Many of his Moulin Rouge pictures had been exhibited in the foyer of the music-hall itself and in the Salon des Indé-pendants. When exhibited as an ensemble in Lautrec's first one-man show (Boussod and Valadon Gallery, 1893), they had a favorable reception. The only leading artist invited to the exhibition was Degas, since his was the only opinion Lautrec valued. Degas came, saw, and approved.

It must not be thought that during this period Lautrec's interests were restricted to music-halls, circuses and popular dance-halls. He continued painting portraits, for example of

QUADRILLE AT THE MOULIN ROUGE, 1892. (31½×23⅞″) ON CARDBOARD. ▶
CHESTER DALE COLLECTION, NATIONAL GALLERY OF ART, WASHINGTON.

In this composition, based on a harmony of deep greens and pinks, Lautrec was evidently more interested in the " figures " of the Quadrille itself than in the individual dancers. The arrangement of the colors stresses the contrast between the bright, vivacious form of the young girl and the somber form of the older woman, whose " invitation to the dance " has a touch of defiance in its wantonness.

Louis Pascal and of Georges-Henri Manuel, their tall, aristocratic figures posed against a studio background.

In 1891 his cousin Gabriel Tapié de Céleyran returned to Paris to complete his medical studies and worked in the hospital where Dr Péan, a magician of the scalpel, was revolutionizing the technique of surgery. Lautrec was allowed to attend his operations, which always drew crowds to see them. Péan drove to the hospital in an open carriage with a coachman and footman in full livery, and operated in a black dress coat with a napkin knotted round his neck to protect his shirt-front. While at work, he favored his audience with a running commentary on the progress of the operation, delivered in a loud, countryfied voice. Lautrec made many pen-and-ink sketches of Péan seen from different angles, and two large pictures, one an over-all view of the operating theater during an operation, the other a close-up showing the operation itself. In the latter, which oddly resembles an enlarged photograph, we see only Péan's face and the patient's throat, on which he is operating.

After those strenuous years 1891-92, devoted to giving a panoramic view of the most colorful and entertaining aspects of the Parisian scene—rounded off by depictions of life in *maisons closes*, its seamy side—he now applied himself to rendering individual types, outstanding personalities of the day.

ALFRED LA GUIGNE, 1894. (25⅞×19¾″) ON CARDBOARD. CHESTER DALE ▶
COLLECTION, NATIONAL GALLERY OF ART, WASHINGTON.

This picture is dedicated to Alfred Méténier and has for its theme a character in a book by that writer, who held an administrative post at a police station and wrote novels about the life of the underworld. Here Lautrec made a synthesis of type-figures he had seen in taverns and houses of ill fame. For the central part of the composition, the broadly rendered garment of the leading figure, he uses the natural tint of the cardboard, restricting more detailed treatment to the faces and the setting, which foreshadow his later interpretations of *L'Assommoir*.

CULT OF THE STAR

LAUTREC watched with interest the careers of the variety artists whom he had known and liked in their Montmartre débuts, and when they were given engagements in the big Paris music-halls and theaters continued to keep in touch with them. Bruant had a season at Les Ambassadeurs where, not long after, Yvette Guilbert (who had attracted attention some years earlier at the Divan Japonais) scored a notable success. In the spring of 1893 Jane Avril did dance turns in the Jardin de Paris, recently installed amongst the trees of the Champs-Elysées. And Loïe Fuller gave her first performances at the Folies-Bergère.

La Goulue incarnated as it were a collective phenomenon, orgiastic dancing at the Moulin Rouge, and once she left the temple of Terpsichore in which she cut an almost hieratic figure, was out of her element and went rapidly downhill. Jane Avril, on the other hand, was at her best when performing a solo turn on a real stage, before a less obstreperous and more attentive audience. She had devised a choreography of her own, composed of graceful side-steps interspersed with sudden whirlwind " spins. " Though she had only a small voice, she included songs in her repertory; but her chief asset was a gift of making the most of her strange physique, her melancholy face, the languid grace of an amazingly supple body.

Lautrec was greatly taken by the slightly perverse appeal of Jane Avril, the creamy whiteness of her skin, her subtle, studied elegance, and he made numerous sketches and pictures of her, dancing, pulling on her gloves, or leaving the Moulin

◄ ARISTIDE BRUANT: POSTER FOR "LES AMBASSADEURS," 1892. (78½×46") MANILA PAPER AND TRACING REMOUNTED ON CANVAS. MUSÉE D'ALBI.

Rouge. When commissioned to make a poster for the Divan Japonais (1892), a small Montmartre music-hall where Yvette Guilbert then was singing, he relegated the singer to the background and gave Jane Avril, in the role of a spectator, accompanied by Edouard Dujardin, the most prominent position. On the cover of *L'Estampe Originale* (1893) he shows her examining a print just pulled by old Cotelle who worked at the Imprimerie Ancourt and was his favorite printer. He had made several preliminary sketches of her wearing a cape and feathered hat, and worked over these assiduously till from the complex tracery of lines there emerged a flawless arabesque. Finally in his much-admired *Jardin de Paris* poster (1893) Lautrec effected a synthesis of all these diverse compositions, showing a command of his material worthy of an old Japanese master.

JANE AVRIL DANCING " LA MELINITE " AT THE MOULIN ROUGE (DETAIL), ▶
1893. ON CARDBOARD. LOUVRE, PARIS.

After being a circus rider and dancing in the Moulin Rouge " Quadrille," Jane Avril did solo turns at the Jardin de Paris, Les Décadents and Le Divan Japonais before scoring her triumphs at the Folies-Bergère and Casino de Paris—and even in the Peer Gynt dances. Lautrec was fascinated by her curious charm, the tense, agonized expression of her face and that creamy-white complexion which is the privilege of red-haired women. Also, he appreciated the taste she showed in dressing; her preference for subtle, sophisticated pale blues and orange-yellows, her little capes and huge, elaborately built hats. His most successful poster (for Le Jardin de Paris) shows her in orange and yellow, waving her long, black-sheathed leg. In the foreground the hand of the double-bass player and the neck of his instrument loom up, prodigiously enlarged, forming a decorative pattern that culminates in the bold distortion of the man's head, making it look like some exotic flower. Its long recessions and contrasted movements differentiate this poster from Bonnard's (for the *Revue Blanche*), which was chiefly an ingenious arrangement of the picture surface.

PAGE 60. PIERRE BONNARD (1867-1947). LA REVUE BLANCHE, 1894.
(31⅜×24¼") POSTER.

PAGE 61. JANE AVRIL AT THE JARDIN DE PARIS, 1893. (21⅜×15¾") POSTER.

For her part, Jane Avril was one of the few variety artists who understood Lautrec, enjoyed his company and took a genuine interest in his work. He saw much of her and when he gave studio parties she often played the hostess. It was by way of Jane Avril that he branched out into the "psychological portrait," a new genre whose great and lasting success was largely due to Lautrec.

In 1893 in collaboration with Ibels he brought out a collection of twenty-two lithographs featuring well-known café-concert artists. Amongst the eleven by his hand were those of Yvette Guilbert, Caudieux, the English *diseuse* Mary Hamilton and that curious woman Mme Abdala, who willfully exaggerated the ugliness of her face. When the music-halls closed in September, Lautrec took to frequenting the Comédie-Française, whose traditionalist, old-world atmosphere quite enchanted him. There is a charming lithograph showing Leloir and Egyptian-profiled Marguerite Moreno (then a pale young girl) in *Les Femmes Savantes*. Also he made a series of drawings for the small magazine named *L'Escarmouche*; then lithographed and published them. The title-page bore the epigraph "I have seen this" directly inspired by Goya's *Disasters of War* (1863, Madrid), for a reprint of which he designed a cover. Within a few months Lautrec had made a remarkably complete pictorial anthology of all that had caught his eye on the Paris stage: the spectacular play *Madame Satan* in which Marcelle Lender scored a triumph, Sarah Bernhardt in *Phèdre*, Mme Caron in

◄ CAUDIEUX, 1893. (44⅞×34½″) SKETCH ON PAPER. MUSÉE D'ALBI.

Lautrec made a poster and several sketches of this café-concert performer, then appearing at the Petit Casino and Les Ambassadeurs. He was obviously struck by the man's superb vulgarity and the terrific vital energy which gave his cumbrous body an air of nimble lightness when he pranced across the stage. This is admirably suggested in the elaborately worked-out sketch in Albi Museum.

63

Faust, Julia Bartet and Mounet-Sully in *Antigone*, Antoine at the Théâtre Libre, Réjane and Galipaux in *Madame Sans-Gêne*, Lugné-Poe and Baldy at the Oeuvre, Brandès and Leloir (his face fantastically made up for his part) in *Cabotins*.

Much as Lautrec enjoyed the spectacular side of the theater, it was on the individual actors that his interest centered. In fact he was one of the first to sponsor that idolization of the " star " which has been carried so far in the English-speaking countries; of the actor who, for good or ill, monopolizes the public's attention, stealing the other players' thunder—but sometimes brings off the miracle of transforming a dull play into a sparkling success.

Joyant describes Lautrec " jotting down his impressions of people in the boxes and lobbies of theaters, touching up his sketches in the intermissions, adding a dab of blue for an eye, a red line for a mouth; drawing, in fact, all the time, no matter where, no matter what the subject. Often a mere dot and a couple of dashes were the jumping-off point for a lithograph or picture... Night after night he went to the same theater, café-concert or music-hall at exactly the same time and sat in the same place, so as to see the bright particular star of the moment in an attitude that had caught his fancy."

In 1894 he suddenly awoke to the great possibilities of Yvette Guilbert as a subject; hitherto he had stressed, rather

LOIE FULLER AT THE FOLIES-BERGÈRE, 1893. (24×17¼″) ON CARDBOARD. ▶
MUSÉE D'ALBI.

Lautrec shows this famous dancer as she appeared on the stage, in an iridescent swirl of gossamer-light veils. Loie Fuller was a plump, pretty young woman of American origin, slightly vulgar and an indifferent actress. Then she had the brilliant idea of launching a new kind of dance, utilizing what was then a relative novelty in Paris, electric light, to flood with changing colors her flimsy skirts held up on sticks. Her dances were a great success and indeed started a new style of dancing. Lautrec made a lithograph of this sketch, in color picked out with gold.

YVETTE GUILBERT BOWING TO THE PUBLIC, 1894. (18⅞×9¾″) PROOF PICKED OUT WITH COLOR MIXED WITH TURPENTINE. MUSÉE D'ALBI.

YVETTE GUILBERT, 1894. ▶ (73×36½″) MANILA PAPER, CHARCOAL AND COLOR. MUSÉE D'ALBI.

Unfailing in his efforts to capture the secrets of Yvette Guilbert's face and attitudes, Lautrec made hosts of preparatory sketches, trying to catch the faint pout of her lips, the exact lift of her eyebrows, the tilt of her nose which, as Jules Renard remarked, " would make things easy if one wanted to kiss her." Lautrec stressed the flaring red of her dyed hair, set off in this hand-colored proof-copy of a lithograph by the green mass of the dress and the pink line across her eyes. Annoyed by his unflattering rendering of her appearance, and encouraged by her mother and Jean Lorrain, who detested Lautrec, Yvette refused the poster. When next year, at her request, Lautrec designed a ceramic with a likeness of her (it was meant to serve as a tea-tray), she wrote on it: " Petit monstre ! Mais vous avez fait une horreur ! "

disdainfully, only the characteristic long black gloves. But now he saw she was a genius in her line and, what was more to the point, how he could turn her ugliness to account by emphasizing it. He designed a poster for her but she turned it down, having already commissioned one from Steinlen. Nor had he better luck with a second attempt; Yvette's friends dissuaded her from employing so brutally candid an artist for a poster meant to attract the public. However, when it came to lithographs she was more amenable. In the course of a boating expedition on the Seine with Lautrec and Gustave Geffroy she agreed to let her two friends make an album, with the text by Geffroy and sixteen lithographs by Lautrec, showing her in various attitudes as she appeared on the stage. Launched by the publisher Marty, the album was a great success.

Now that his projects for posters had fallen through, Lautrec was devoting himself more and more to lithography (in black and in color) and scaling down the poster to the size and lay-out of the lithograph. Amongst these reduced-scale posters for indoors use, masterpieces of their kind, were those inspired by May Belfort, May Milton and Jeanne Granier *(Confetti)*, all executed with a striking economy of means. Thus the only color in the first is the rich red of the performer's dress; while in the second, on the other hand, the dominant note is struck by the blue ground. In *Confetti* there is a careless rapture in the line, an ethereal lightness in the composition, while the face has become pure glamour, the smiling grace of youth incarnate.

CONFETTI, 1894. (21¼×15¾″) POSTER. ▶

Joyant describes this poster, designed for a confetti factory, as " built up around Jeanne Granier's smile." Here the composition of the figure, all on the surface, the planes being suggested solely by displacements of the line, reminds one of Bonnard. But the bold drawing of the hands showering tiny flakes of color is typically Lautrec's.

69

"AU SALON"

Most of the not inconsiderable part of Lautrec's œuvre which deals with the life of the Parisian prostitute dates to 1894. As a matter of fact he had taken to visiting houses of ill fame several years before. For in these places he found, as Mac Orlan puts it, " both forgetfulness of his appearance and that unsophisticated, rudimentary type of talk which acts like a healing silence."

His friend Bruant used to seek inspiration in the company of prostitutes; they " gave him ideas." But Lautrec had a real fellow-feeling for them; they, *too*, had had no luck in life. He had almost a " fixation " on red-haired women and the creamy white skin that often goes with red hair. His earliest model, " the washerwoman," and nearly all of the girls who posed for him in Forest's gardens could boast of exceptionally fine hair. Her russet hair was " Mme Poupoule's " redeeming feature and he submerged her face in it in his portrait of her. Also, Lautrec found a curious charm in the unnatural pallor of the women cloistered in the *maisons closes*, and their worn-out, flaccid bodies in which the flame of life burnt low.

To adorn the " salon " of an establishment of this kind in the Rue d'Amboise he painted a suite of medallions of the

◀ THE SALON IN THE RUE DES MOULINS (DETAIL), 1894. ON CANVAS. MUSÉE D'ALBI.

This big canvas depicting the " oriental room " at the bawdyhouse in the Rue des Moulins is a synthesis of Lautrec's careful studies of the life and mores of French prostitutes. He has grouped on sofas the inmates, whose various attitudes he knows so well, and their air of lackadaisical indifference gives a sort of uniformity to the ensemble. There is one exception, the *sous-maîtresse*, Madame's understudy, who is sitting primly erect in a tight-fitting dress and whose features have a curious sharpness.

71

women there, with coiffures in the Louis XV style and their profiles fined down into graceful arabesques. In 1894 he became a paying guest in a de-luxe establishment in the Rue des Moulins and made studies for the set of lithographs named *Elles*, as well as portraits of the women there, Marcelle, Rolande, Gabrielle, Lucie Bellanger, and Mme Baron, who were to reappear in many of his pictures. He also painted the owners of the place and members of the staff. Finally, from this material he built up methodically, painstakingly, in the calm of his studio the big group composition named *Au Salon*.

Lautrec was not the first artist to find a source of inspiration in houses of ill fame. Constantin Guys and Degas had already made some memorable compositions on these themes. Always interested in the wonderful diversity of forms and attitudes to be observed in women's bodies, Degas had studied the prostitute from the same angle as his ballet dancers. Guys' approach was more factual; he stressed the women's idiosyncrasies and showed them plying their trade; thus his pictures are almost " documentaries " of the life of the Parisian prostitute. In the work of Lautrec, however (though he participated far more closely in these women's lives), there is not the least trace of sensuality or any suggestion of eroticism. He depicts the life of the professional prostitutes with ruthless, even clinical precision, treating it almost as if it were a natural, normal mode of existence. He shows them on view in their " Salon," having their meals, in bed side by side, but never with the slightest allusion to their trade or to their clientèle. He is always objective; never moralizes, never criticizes, and dramatizes nothing.

The curiously static atmosphere of the *maison close*, in which life seemed in abeyance and the human element mere inert matter offered to his scrutiny, appealed to him. In Paris he used to take up his abode for days at a time in houses of this order, receiving friends there, and in fact making himself thoroughly at home. When visiting Bordeaux, instead of putting up in an hotel, he always stayed in a *maison close* in the Rue Pessac, where he had booked a room in advance. On these occasions he presided at the " family " luncheon, to which he made generous contributions in the form of drinks and delicacies, and guided the course of the conversation, which he was careful to keep on a level of amiability and indeed decorum that he was far from maintaining, himself, when in the company of his high-society friends. On their days off he took the girls for outings, often to the theater, always treating them with friendly courtesy.

During these visits he was treated like one of the family and had the run of the house. He often took his morning coffee with the girls, joined in their card games, encouraged them to confide in him, and occasionally paid them surprise visits when they were in bed—sometimes two or three in the same bed. To his mind they were the perfect models. " The professional model is always like a stuffed owl," he once said. " These girls are alive." They provided him (as they provided Degas) with glimpses of nudity or semi-nudity at its freest; under ideal conditions, that is to say, from the artist's point of view.

Every human institution, however much looked down on, or even degrading, has a functional value that ennobles it. The world of prostitution which, when we view it from the sociological angle, seems so ignoble and revolting, is of much interest to the student of human nature; for it has type-figures, customs and even ethics of its own—in fact, a code of morals defying everyday morality. And it held even more interest for the artist who elected to live within it, to study it with an open mind and an observant eye. There is no sensuality, no pity or sentimentalism in Lautrec's work; it is a faithful record, precise not picturesque. Yet somehow the persons he depicts, rising above their human situation, achieve a universal significance.

THE SALON IN THE RUE DES MOULINS (STUDY FOR THE PRECEDING PICTURE), 1894. (43⅝ × 51⅞") PASTEL. MUSÉE D'ALBI.

This pastel sketch for the picture a detail of which is given elsewhere shows the artist's careful handling of chromatic elements. The faces stand out against rich, vivid colors or, in the case of Madame's " second-in-command," a brilliant white. The canvas, on the other hand, is bathed in an ambience of mauve and faded pink, evoking the general atmosphere of the " house," its curious remoteness from everyday life.

WOMAN PULLING ON HER STOCKING, 1894. (23½ × 16⅞") MUSÉE D'ALBI. ▶

Like all true revolutionaries, Lautrec was at once greatly daring and at the same time reluctant to give needless offense. He kept to himself all the pictures dealing with this subject, which are not only of paramount importance in his œuvre, but constitute one of its most original and novel features; yet though quite conscious that he had rarely, if ever produced better work, he showed them only to a few friends. When he gave an exhibition at the Manzi-Joyant Gallery in 1896, he kept these pictures in a locked room to which he admitted only visitors who approached him personally. Most of these works (which remained in his studio until his death) can now be seen in the museum at Albi. Actually there is nothing in them that can shock or give offense to the modern observer, however it may have been fifty years ago; their utter truthfulness and purity of forms surely entitle them to a high and lasting place in the world's art. Indeed these glimpses of women washing or pulling on their stockings are of all time and of no time. Even in the pictures which (like that amazing synthesis, *Au Salon*) bring home to us most clearly what the " oldest profession in the world " was like in Lautrec's day, what is there to which any of us can take exception? Though the period when they were painted is relatively near, we can hardly discern today, even on a close study of the costumes and the setting, what associates them with that period and that profession; and when but a few more years have passed, all that the discriminating eye will see in them is a noble counterpoint of rhythms and forms.

THE WASHERMAN. ▶

Lautrec recorded the life of the establishment in the Rue des Moulins under all its daily aspects. This one is characteristic: the washerman's haggard, sallow face furrowed by hard toil and illness (this man, whom Lautrec knew well, was consumptive) and, confronting it, the plump, rubicund face of " Madame " consulting her washing-list.

THE WASHERMAN, 1894. (26¼×17⅝") ON CARDBOARD.
MUSÉE D'ALBI.

78

THE THEATER - NEW FRIENDSHIPS

LAUTREC was at the height of his powers in 1895-1896 and these were his most prolific years. Though his major works were rarely to be seen outside his studio, his name was, thanks to his posters and lithographs, becoming familiar to the general public. Moreover, he was much esteemed by the artists of the new generation. And the circle of his friends now included famous authors of the day as well as the literary, political and fashionable élite gravitating around the *Revue Blanche*.

In 1895 Lautrec continued his survey of the world of the music-hall and theater, and produced vast synthetic compositions in which he proved his definitive mastery of these themes; but, by the same token, that he had exhausted their possibilities. For *Le Rire* he did some drawings of Polaire who, with her immense eyes, knife-edged smile and almost incredible verve, was having a big success at Les Ambassadeurs. He became infatuated with a young Irish singer, May Belfort, then doing (at " Les Décadents ") a turn much like that of Jane Avril, whose style of dressing—dainty capelines, high-waisted frocks—she copied. While singing, she held a little cat in her arms, or let her arms dangle limply at her side, and never moved at all. In the glare of the footlights her pallor and strongly accentuated features made her seem like a visitant from another world. Lautrec painted her again and again, with slight variations, before making five lithographs of her (only one was issued) and a poster for her performances at the Petit Casino. Thereafter he continued seeing her, and designed for her a menu and a greetings card for 1897.

◀ DOCTOR GABRIEL TAPIÉ DE CÉLEYRAN IN A CORRIDOR AT THE COMÉDIE FRANÇAISE, 1894. (43¼ × 22″) ON CANVAS. MUSÉE D'ALBI.

Another English dancer, May Milton, asked him to make a poster for her American tour. One of his best works in this genre, it makes the most of her childish face, flaxen hair, and the bright mass of her frock standing out against a blue ground. Picasso owned this poster when he came to Paris and we see it hanging on the wall of his studio in *The Blue Room* (1901).

Lautrec was often to be seen in the English bars around the Madeleine; particularly the Cosmopolitan run by Picton in Rue Scribe and the Irish and American Bar presided over by Ralph the barman. May Belfort and May Milton often had supper at these places, and it may have been they who took him there to start with. The customers figuring in a poster (1896) and the scene of *Chocolat Dancing* are obviously jockeys, stable-lads and rich folks' coachmen. Lautrec was so much taken by the plump, square-cut, impassive face of Tom, the Rothschilds' coachman, that he worked him into the composition of *La Grande Loge*, top-hat and all. The clowns Footit and Chocolat were appearing at the Nouveau Cirque, where Lautrec made some striking drawings of the former dressed as a *danseuse* (one appeared in *Le Rire*, January 26, 1895). With his muscular frame and cruel face, this clown, who was never seen to laugh, got his comic effects solely by the contrast with his opposite number Chocolat, who played the part of a harmless long-suffering imbecile. Lautrec's drawing of Chocolat (1896) brings out the marvelous agility behind the colored dancer's seeming lethargy.

MAY BELFORT, 1895. (23½ × 14¾″) ON CARDBOARD. G. RENAND ▶
COLLECTION, PARIS.

Though her face was that of a grown woman, this Irish singer always wore little-girl frocks, and, dandling a black kitten in her arms, sang childish songs such as " Daddy wouldn't buy me a bow-wow," to tickle the jaded palates of the habitués of the Café des Décadents, the Jardin de Paris, Olympia and the Petit Casino.

Lautrec's contacts with the Moulin Rouge had not yet ended. On April 6, 1895, he had a message from La Goulue, whom he had not seen for two years, asking if he would paint decorations for the booth in which she was now reduced to exhibiting herself, at traveling fairs. He had always wanted to do mural painting and at once consented. On a coarse canvas he painted two big pictures, one representing the past—La Goulue in the Moulin Rouge Quadrille—, the other the present day—La Goulue dressed as an Egyptian dancing-girl. In the foreground he grouped as her audience a number of well-known figures of the 'nineties, amongst them Fénéon and Oscar Wilde. These pictures were ready and in place as early as the beginning of July.

Lautrec happened to be in London during Oscar Wilde's first trial, and the author of *Dorian Gray*, then at the height of his fame and the pet of London society, fancied his position secure enough for him to defy the British moral code. Wilde, who had met Lautrec in Paris some years before, refused to sit for his portrait, but the painter " caught him on the wing " as Joyant puts it. With a fine economy of means he shows us the pallid, puffy face, like that of some huge nightbird with a blood-red mouth, against a faintly indicated background of the tower of Westminster and the Thames. And surely no more poignant illustration exists of the drama taking place that day in London!

DECORATION OF LA GOULUE'S BOOTH, DETAIL: FÉLIX FÉNÉON. 1895. ▶
LOUVRE, PARIS.

Looking at La Goulue dressed as an Egyptian dancer, with Sescau accompanying her on the piano, are Oscar Wilde, Guibert and Félix Fénéon, whose gaunt, glabrous face is shown in profile. When on the staff of *Le Matin*, Fénéon had got Lautrec commissions for making posters for the serials running in that newspaper *(Le Pendu)*. Fénéon had just come out of prison, after being arrested during the anarchist trials, and was now sub-editor of the *Revue Blanche*.

83

The Nouveau Cirque was the scene of the exploits of the oddly named woman-clown Cha-U-Kao who inspired some of Lautrec's finest pictures of this period. Her personality would remain a mystery, were it not so well brought out by the cast of her unsmiling face, the white wig crowned with a bunch of yellow ribbons matching the flimsy collarette floating round her shoulders. Lautrec has shown her in her dressing-room, unfastening the collarette and displaying the wide sweep of her brawny shoulders (Louvre); also strolling in the lounge of the Moulin Rouge. In 1896 she presided on horseback at a burlesque *ridotto* at the Moulin Rouge; in our last glimpse of her, a colored lithograph, she is seated, wearing a look of sadness which redeems the coarseness of her face.

It was in 1895 that Lautrec's interest in the theater took its most active form. He designed programs for several plays: in January, for *Le Chariot de Terre Cuite*, based on an Indian legend, at the Œuvre (he also collaborated with Valtat for the sets); in March, for Tristan Bernard's *Les Pieds Nickelés*; in May, for Fabre's *L'Argent*. For several weeks he was under the spell of Marcelle Lender whom he regarded as " the most wonderful creature he had ever seen on the stage." On January 1 she had begun appearing in Hervé's light opera *Chilpéric* (a burlesque in the style of *La Belle Hélène*), singing and doing Spanish dances. In her Memoirs she tells how Edwards brought Jules Renard and Lautrec (whom she had not met before) to the Café Viel, where she was having supper after the show.

CHA-U-KAO, THE " CLOWNESS." ▶

This young woman performed at the Nouveau Cirque and was often to be seen at the Moulin Rouge. In his many pictures of her Lautrec gives her an air of majestic melancholy and here the thickly powdered face under a white *toupet* has something of the pensive sadness of Jane Avril. The bearded man on the right is Tristan Bernard. This picture was bought by King Milan of Serbia, who, after his dethronment, lived in Paris.

CHA-U-KAO, THE " CLOWNESS," 1895.
(29 ½ × 21 ½") ON CANVAS.
DR OSKAR REINHART COLLECTION, WINTERTHUR.

CHA-U-KAO SEATED, 1896. (20¾ × 15⅞″) COLOR LITHOGRAPH. GIFT OF
MRS JOHN D. ROCKEFELLER, JR., MUSEUM OF MODERN ART, NEW YORK.

Lautrec talked to her about the circus, was charming, gay, came back on three consecutive nights, and one evening sent her a bouquet of white roses after the fandango of Act II. He lunched with her once at her home and looked her up in her dressing-room at the theater several times. She never saw him take out a pencil or make the briefest note. Two months later the picture was completed without his having said a word about it.

Seemingly the freest of his compositions, this actually is one of the most carefully thought out. The central figure, the only one that is alive and expressive, sets the rhythm, borne out by the slant given each of the other carefully posed figures. The white patches formed by faces illuminated by the footlights are streaked with greenish or bluish shadows, and the general effect is a subtle harmony of pink and green. Intricate though it is, and an " essential " work, this picture was done in a sudden gust of inspiration; as usual Lautrec followed up with several versions of the details, lithographs showing Lender dancing the bolero, and (half-length) bowing.

In the same year Lautrec brought out a second album of lithographs (black-and-white) of actors and actresses. This is a rather puzzling work, for there is a curious ambiguity about the figures; it is no easy matter deciding whom they are meant to represent. In fact opinions differ widely regarding several prints. Have we here Sarah Bernhardt or Mademoiselle Sabra; Eve Lavallière or Polaire or Emilienne d'Alençon; Yvette Guilbert or Lender; Cassive or Jeanne Hading? There is less uncertainty about the likenesses of Cléo de Mérode, Jeanne Granier, Lucien Guitry (in the new play *Amants* at La Renaissance) and Polin. One would almost think Lautrec wanted to create a sort of grotesque kinship between all these players. For the distortions are not due solely to the stage lighting, but are willfully exaggerated.

MARCELLE LENDER IN THE BOLERO OF " CHILPERIC," 1895-1896. (58×59")
ON CANVAS. BY COURTESY OF MR JOHN HAY WHITNEY, NEW YORK,
(OPPOSITE PAGE: HEAD OF MARCELLE LENDER, DETAIL.)

Outcome of many years' study of the life of the theater, as seen both
from the stalls and behind the scenes, this picture shows Lautrec at his
dazzling best. Night after night for weeks he attended performances of
Chilperic, so as to steep himself as it were in Marcelle Lender's personality.
Everything about her charmed him: her elegance, her vivacity, the lithe
grace of her moving body, from the rippling hair to the twinkling ankles.
As for her back, he " had never seen anything so splendid." Later, he
used her face again in one of his most famous color lithographs.

It was now that Lautrec enlarged his circle of friends. He had always had a little group of boon companions, mostly bachelors like himself, who never left his side by day or night. Though he was exacting, indeed tyrannical, in his demands on them, his personal charm, his tact and wit were such that they, one and all, were utterly devoted to him. Each had his appropriate function in Lautrec's little court; his tall cousin Gabriel de Céleyran was so to speak the Lord Chamberlain, master of the revels; Maurice Guibert, a traveler in champagne, the court buffoon and butt. Lautrec made drawings of him in the most ridiculous situations, chasing girls along the waterfront at Bordeaux, or warbling sentimental ditties. Dujardin, poet, music critic and a great Wagner enthusiast, was the most spectacular figure, with his long flowing beard, his monocle and his elegant poise. Needless to say, there was always Joyant, the painter's lifelong friend. Now, however, a new batch of friends, mostly connected with the *Revue Blanche*, joined the Old Guard: Tristan Bernard, Félix Fénéon, Romain Coolus, Paul Leclercq. Similarly, the painter friends of his student days—Anquetin, the two Alberts, Gauzi and Grenier—now were joined by Bonnard, Vuillard, Vallotton and notably Maxime Dethomas, all of whom Lautrec (only a few years their senior) treated with the greatest kindness and whose work he tried to get his friends to buy.

The *Revue Blanche* group stood for the boldest, most advanced ideas of the day in literature, politics and art; the Natanson brothers had created around them an atmosphere of

MAXIME DETHOMAS. ▶

What Lautrec liked best at the Opera was the annual masked ball; in 1897 he acted as one of the judges of the costumes. He made this the setting for his likenesses of the Prince de Sagan, M. Fourcade and the painter-graver Dethomas. Dethomas' placidity, corpulence and extreme shyness (he always blushed when he had to raise his voice) endeared him to Lautrec.

MAXIME DETHOMAS, 1896. (26½ × 21″) ON CARDBOARD. CHESTER DALE
COLLECTION, NATIONAL GALLERY OF ART, WASHINGTON.

youth, adventurousness and wit, and Lautrec greatly valued their friendship. It was above all in 1895 and the following years, when the review had moved into premises in the Rue Laffitte, that Lautrec, who had been preceded by Vuillard, Bonnard and Roussel, became a leading figure of the group.

Alexandre Natanson's wife was an actress, Marthe Mellot, for whom subsequently Lautrec made one of his best posters, *La Gitane* (1900). Thadée Natanson was married to Missia Godebski, daughter of a Polish refugee sculptor; she was a cultivated woman and a fine musician, and Lautrec greatly liked her. He used her as his model for a poster made for the review in 1895, showing the small face, with its assured if rather inscrutable expression, peeping through a mist of feathers, furs and veils. Later, he painted her playing the piano, and in her garden. When he was under treatment in the mental hospital at Neuilly she came to see him and her visits always had beneficial effects. Very few of the women he admired could understand him; most were merely intrigued, sometimes amused, and soon had had enough of him. It was probably " our radiant, sibylline Missia " as Lugné-Poe called her, who felt nearest him.

The Natansons, who entertained lavishly, always insisted on Lautrec's being present at their parties. One famous occasion was the inauguration of a reception-room decorated by Vuillard. Lautrec, who had organized everything, officiated as barman, in a white coat, and handed out to the guests mixed drinks of an extraordinary potency, though himself, for once in the way, keeping as sober as a judge. When staying at the Natansons' country house at Villeneuve-sur-Yonne, Lautrec rose early, went swimming in the river and displayed his prowess as an oarsman. During one of these visits he planned a series of aphorisms on bachelordom in collaboration with Cipa Godebski. It was at the Natansons' country place that

BERTHE BADY, 1897. (27×22¾″) ON CARDBOARD. MUSÉE D'ALBI.

This actress was a close friend of Henry Bataille. Lautrec was much
taken by the vivacity of her gaze and the expressiveness of her mouth,
emphasized here by a dextrous arrangement of tapering lines.

CHOCOLAT DANCING IN ACHILLE'S BAR, 1896. (30¼×24″) INDIAN INK
AND BLUE CRAYON WITH TOUCHES OF WHITE. MUSÉE D'ALBI.

Vuillard painted the two fine portraits of Lautrec which are now in the museum at Albi.

Lautrec was much attracted to Tristan Bernard, whose simple, unaffected manners delighted him. Bernard, who then was managing the " Buffalo " cycle-track, took Lautrec behind the scenes of the world of boxing and cycle-racing. As a matter of fact Lautrec was less interested in the actual prize-fights and races than in the training of the champions and the activities of their satellites. Bouglé, Paris representative of the " Simpson Chain," became one of his closest friends. Lautrec went to London with the racing cyclists working for that firm and came back with two sketches for posters; *The Michael Cycle* (so named after a Welsh cycling champion) and *The Simpson Chain*. Lautrec also made a painting of Bernard on his cycle-track. But these new departures did not divert him from his old pursuits; in 1896 he published the album of lithographs named *Elles*. He also had an idea of illustrating the Goncourts' *La Fille Elisa*, and did a number of admirable watercolors on Maurice Joyant's copy. But he soon tired of following the text and made, instead, a series of plates on the lives of the women in a " house. " None of these is named or numbered; five are in colors, five merely on a tinted ground. Some are new interpretations of a detail or a face in one of the earlier paintings, while others, those representing almost repulsive figures, have none the less a tranquil grandeur of their own. There are also some nudes, of a rare, poignant beauty.

◀ CHOCOLAT DANCING IN ACHILLE'S BAR.

In this study for an illustration in *Le Rire* (March 28, 1896) Lautrec shows us the colored partner of the British clown Footit whose performances were making a great hit at the Nouveau Cirque. In the ring the capering, " rubber-legged " antics of Chocolat in red trousers and black coat provided an effective foil to the angular primness of Footit dressed as a pantomime " dame." This sketch brings out well the extraordinary litheness and muscular development of the colored dancer's body.

AT THE BAR: THE CHLOROTIC CASHIER, 1898. (32¼×23½")
ON CARDBOARD. KUNSTHAUS, ZURICH.

OLD THEMES : NEW INTERPRETATIONS

LAUTREC got from drink (as Natanson puts it) "the nervous tension which seems like dynamism, feverish excitement that takes itself for joy." He did not drink, as some have thought, in order to forget his physical condition, but because drink whipped up his zest for life. Drinkers figure in some of his earliest work and he could count on seeing in the innumerable cafés of Paris, whether smart or sordid (he frequented both impartially), human types that appealed to him by reason of the fixity of their attitudes, the monumental calm most men develop at a certain stage of drunkenness.

The trouble was that as time went on he had to drink more and more to get the desired effect. As for food, he had a sophisticated palate and a talent for concocting highly spiced dishes, so delicious that Parisian *chefs* were glad to have the recipes and Joyant even made a book of them. Also he appreciated vintage wines, especially full-bodied Burgundies, and was a connoisseur of port, cognac and champagne. He liked cocktails for their prompt and perilous effects, but, when the craving came, even the coarsest forms of alcohol, inferior rum and *marc*, served his turn. Indeed in these latter years he ceased to be discriminating—any drink would do, provided there was plenty of it—and he got into the way of being almost always in a semi-fuddled state, which his friends, broken in to his habits, came to take for granted.

His character changed; losing the self-command which had been one of his assets, he became crotchety, querulous, quick to fly into a temper. His appearance also changed; his eyes, once crystal-clear, acquired the fogginess characteristic of the habitual drinker. He now spoke more jerkily, truncating words to the point of unintelligibility and interspersing them with vague grunts. For weeks on end he ceased working at all. Sometimes, realizing what was happening, he tried going to the country or traveling, in the hope of breaking his habits. When he moved into his new studio (15, Avenue Frochot) and invited his friends to the house-warming, all he offered them was cups of milk—the motif of a charming lithographed invitation card.

For some weeks he made a bar in the Rue Bréda, patronized by Lesbians, his headquarters and did several paintings of Palmyre who ran the place and also of her particularly ugly bulldog " Bouboule " who had a habit of nipping the lady customers' legs, presumably out of jealousy. There he seemed quite at home in an atmosphere of alcohol and ether, surrounded by a bevy of languid women in masculine attire, starched collars and ties.

He still stayed occasionally in houses of ill fame, along with Romain Coolus, whom he had reduced to a state of absolute subjection. He now made another series of large nudes, using a red-haired model whom he showed standing at her mirror, or kneeling on furs (a posture inspired by an illustration he once had made for Zola's *La Curée*). In these elaborately worked-out pictures the rather finicky precision of the drawing is compensated for by the dashing brushwork, and in the slashes of red and green mottling the woman's flesh we have a sort of expressive disintegration of color. Another work of this period is *La Sphynge*, a vision of sheer sensuality, bathed in a phosphorescent sheen. And finally,

MADAME POUPOULE AT HER TOILET. ▶

In a kind of pale blue négligé, resting her arms on her dressing-table, Madame Poupoule is wisely hiding most of her rather banal face behind a mass of glorious red hair. Remarkable in this portrait is the meticulous attention, rare with Lautrec, given to rendering the smallest details; e.g. the play of light on the hands, glints of reflected color in the bottles.

MADAME POUPOULE AT HER TOILET, 1898. (23 ½ × 15 ¾")
ON WOOD. MUSÉE D'ALBI.

Madame Poupoule stands for the culmination of his experiments in the handling of pigment, with its use of broken, iridescent colors to render the textures of hair, garments and even the wall in the background.

He also made several portraits, mostly in the setting of his studio, notable for their unity of style and the *finesse* of their execution. One was that of M. de Lauradour, whose red beard and huge body fascinated him; another that of Nocq, a small, bilious-looking goldsmith whom he painted twice, once in a cloak, bare-headed and, again, wearing a bowler (the quiet humor of these portraits was not relished by the sitter); and, lastly, of Paul Leclercq: a work whose elegance and subtlety remind us of some 18th-century portraits.

Leclercq, who presented this picture to the Louvre, has recorded some interesting facts about Lautrec's methods of work. " I realized how amazing was his talent when I was sitting for my portrait. For a month I came regularly three or four times a week to his studio, but I am quite sure I didn't ' sit ' for him more than two or three times all told. The moment I came in he waved me into a big wicker arm-chair, then took his stand at the easel, wearing the soft felt hat he always kept on in his studio. Then he leveled his pince-nez at me, screwed up his eyes, took up his brush and after having seen what he wanted, made a few dabs of much-diluted paint on the canvas. After a moment he put down the brush and said peremptorily: ' That's enough for today. It's much too fine outside.' So out we went for a stroll in the nearby streets."

It was in much the same manner (though not quite so casually) that he went about his open-air portraits of the years 1890-1901, which, in their turn, were a continuation of procedures he had worked out for himself in his youth. Indeed this period was marked by a second blooming of the art of his young days. Almost automatically and with unfailing accuracy his mind's eye and his hand retrieved the themes which he had so well mastered in the past: men and women on horseback, jockeys, showy turn-outs—hardly modified at all by the experience acquired in the interim. Thus when Vollard asked him to contribute to his " Album of Painter-Gravers " he produced *The English Dogcart* and, in the same spirit, *The Tandem*, showing a trap bowling merrily along with a dog, looking like an animated lump of fur, dashing ahead, and an almost Japanese landscape for background. He often looked up Bail, the coach-builder, to inspect the latest types of carriages. As he had trouble in walking he hired a trap from his neighbor Calmèse in the Rue Fontaine, who supplied a pony rejoicing in the name of Philibert, " gimlet-eyed and with a belly like a roly-poly," as he put it, " to trundle my old carcass around."

Lautrec had a sympathetic understanding of horses and birds and in the dark phase of his life, haunted by the phantoms of his sick imagination, which he now was entering, his early love for animals returned. He had long had the idea of illustrating Jules Renard's *Histoires Naturelles*, and he now put it into execution (the book was published in January 1899, by Floury). In these illustrations, at once so delicate and so wittily allusive, Lautrec was obviously setting out to equal the lightness of touch and subtle artistry of the masters of the Far East—and we may say that he succeeded, though at first the book was not appreciated as it should have been. Leclercq who accompanied him on his frequent visits to the Zoological Gardens tells us how the painter would spend hours beside a great ant-eater that had got to know him and started jumping for joy when he approached. He also liked monkeys, penguins and (oddly enough) the shrill cries of parrots.

In the years 1897-1898 Lautrec sometimes achieved a still greater objectivity, a still more lucid insight, and, despite ill-health and the ravages of drink, he scaled new heights. But painting now cost him such an effort—for he was never satisfied with anything short of the very best—that his output inevitably dwindled.

He now was making hardly any lithographs, but trying out another art technique ensuring greater accuracy combined with a strict economy of means. His friend Charles Maurin, who had previously shown Lautrec some of the more recondite procedures of lithography, now taught him dry-point etching, and he made portraits of several friends in this medium: Francis Jourdain, Maurin himself, Tristan Bernard, Henri Somm and de Brettes, the explorer. Sands, an English publisher, commissioned a new Yvette Guilbert album; in this he handled her peculiar appearance more leniently than in the past. In 1898 Lautrec gave his first one-man show in London, at the Goupil Gallery. One of the visitors to the exhibition was the Prince of Wales (subsequently King Edward VII), who had been to the Moulin Rouge and met La Goulue. Lautrec was sound asleep when his royal visitor arrived; the Prince smiled and said " Don't wake him !"

Early in 1899 it became more and more evident that Lautrec was heading for a serious breakdown. He fancied himself beset by enemies and conspiracies, saw weird animals, non-existent dogs and swarms of flies. When in bed he kept his stick beside him ready for any emergency. After a particularly bad attack, which took place in public, his mother had him transferred (on March 17) to the sanatorium of

" CLOWNESS. " THE CIRCUS, NO. 7. PASTEL DRAWING. ▶

André Lhote remarks that in the set of drawings named " The Circus " Lautrec aims at giving back to forms the qualities he had deprived them of when he abandoned plastic values. " Bodies now have weight and bulk; he floods them with light and hardens their outlines. No empty spaces remain, except between figures." And Lhote mentions in this context Urs Graf, Daumier and Dürer.

Dr Samelaigne at Neuilly. After a phase of fits of violent rage and extreme depression (it was now he sent that pathetic letter begging his father to procure his release), Lautrec pulled himself together and resolved, by showing himself in full command of his powers as an artist, to prove that there was no need to keep him in confinement. With this in view he made a portrait of his male nurse and the series of pastel drawings named *The Circus*, in which he gave proof of a marvelous visual memory in his renderings of the various turns that had impressed him most in the old days. His friends were amazed by the accuracy of his evocations of the displays of " the higher horsemanship " at Molier's riding-school and by the Baronne de Radhern (the " Baudelairian equestrienne " as Jules Lemaître called her); of a girl acrobat who had performed at the Jardin de Paris ten years before, her yellow tights vividly contrasting with the green darkness of the leafage; of the bear " Caviar "; of Footit and Chocolat. Thanks to this prodigious feat of memory and will-power Lautrec was allowed to regain his liberty. His incarceration had been the signal for a malicious press campaign against the artist. Some journalists spoke of his " madness " as accounting for the distortions and the peculiarities of his art which had always baffled them, and to these attacks Lautrec's friends riposted vigorously in the press. But the absolute accuracy and the sobriety of the *Circus* drawings were *per se* sufficient proof of the artist's sanity.

This escape into the past was the only form of escape that Lautrec ever managed to indulge in. For foreign travel had always been one of his dreams; when at the Café Weber, he often sat in what was called the " Africans' Corner," and, listening to their reminiscences, toyed with the idea of a trip to the Congo. Yearly he gave himself the illusion of a voyage oversea when, for his summer vacation at Arcachon, he went to Le Havre and embarked on a tramp steamer carrying Belgian coal to Bordeaux. Often he and Guibert or Joyant were the only passengers; he practically took command of the ship and made the captain hug the coast of Brittany so that he could buy from Breton fishermen the crayfish needed for the Gargantuan *bouillabaisses* he concocted. On one occasion (1896) there was a lady passenger bound for Dakar on board, and Lautrec was so much struck by her beauty (she figured later in his poster for the " Salon des Cent," *La Passagère du 54*) that he decided to accompany her to Dakar. But when they put in at Lisbon, Guibert refused to go further; so the two friends left the ship and came back through Spain. At Madrid and Toledo Lautrec saw for the first time, in all its splendor, the work of El Greco, the painter he most admired, next to Cranach and Uccello.

After leaving the sanatorium in May 1899 he stayed some weeks in Paris before going to Arcachon, as usual *via* Le Havre. While waiting for his boat he discovered in the " Star," one of the local taverns, a golden-haired young English barmaid whose beauty and vivacity charmed him so much that he promptly telegraphed Joyant to send on his painting outfit. He then painted the famous picture now in the museum at Albi; though a portrait, it has all the movement and sparkle of the large " Moulin Rouge " and " Chilperic " compositions.

From now on Lautrec was always escorted by a certain Monsieur Viaud—" my Barnum " he called him—who, ostensibly an ordinary friend, was there to prevent his drinking. Was it, one wonders, the effect of being deprived of stimulants ? The fact remains that, except on rare occasions such as his encounter with the barmaid at the " Star," he never succeeded in regaining the atmosphere of his early works—or, indeed, his zest for painting. However, he made a few portraits in the course of the winter: of Coolus, Octave Raquin (whom he

nicknamed " Shavings " because of his very fair hair), Mlle
Nys and Mlle Le Margouin (helpmate of his old friend
Adolphe Albert). In this last picture, *La Modiste* (Albi Museum),
the vividly illuminated face and fair hair of the model, and
her bodice with its yellow frill, form a counterpoint of high-
pitched, astringent tones. For the most part, however, Lautrec
now reverted to old subjects, such as racecourse scenes. He
made new versions of *Madame Poupoule at her Toilet*. But he had
difficulty in recapturing the vibrant life so characteristic of his
earlier art and these much worked-over pictures seem curiously
leaden-hued.

In the spring of 1900 he went with Joyant to his home
at Le Crotoy on the Somme estuary. The big portrait of his
friend he now embarked on called for no less than seventy
sittings. Lautrec posed him in the attitude of a hunter on the
watch, in yellow oilskins and sou'wester, a lonely figure
standing out against a blue-green expanse of sea and a narrow
strip of grey sky, with a white sail in the background. Lautrec
used only neutral tints and, though he took infinite pains over
this portrait, it gives an impression of indecision and flim-
siness most unusual in his work.

In June Lautrec returned to the South West of France and
during the last year of his life he rarely ventured far from Malromé where his mother lived. He rented a studio at Bordeaux

THE ENGLISH BARMAID AT THE " STAR," 1899. (16⅛ × 12¾") ON WOOD ▶
MUSÉE D'ALBI.

Lautrec often went to Le Havre to catch the mailboat to Bordeaux, and
did the round of the café-concerts, in which it was then the custom to
employ English barmaids. This particular barmaid, "Miss Dolly,"
impressed him so much that he made this superb portrait in which we
hardly know what to admire most: the expression of the young woman's
face, the golden curls, the harmony between the pink trimming and the
dark blue of the bodice, or the striking color scheme of the background,
a geometrical fantasia in various shades of green, blue and violet.

for the winter and something of the old creative urge came back when he attended the performances of *Messalina*, a tragic opera by Armand Silvestre and Isidore de Lara, in the magnificent Bordeaux Opera House. Once again he was thrilled by the elaborate lighting effects, the gorgeous costumes, the opulent forms of the singers, the colorful evolutions of the chorus. He made a series of drawings and paintings in which he stressed the static, plastic values of the spectacle, by playing off large masses against each other. And, following on this, in April, he tried his hand at sculpture.

In May and June he spent some weeks in Paris, where he made a portrait of André Rivoire (Musée du Petit Palais). " He seems to have had a presentiment," Joyant writes, " that the end was near. He put his canvases and sketches in order, and though for years he had never even glanced at the contents of the loft above his studio, he now went through them carefully. He endorsed with his monogram and signed all the works which to his thinking did him justice." *An Examination at the Faculty of Medicine*, the last big composition he undertook, was never completed; it marked the culmination of his technical evolution, being painted in broad strokes of expressive color, masses replacing linework.

In July Lautrec left for Bordeaux and Arcachon. He painted a large sketch of Viaud, as an 18th-century admiral on his flagship. Abruptly stricken with paralysis, he was taken to Malromé. " He watched everything but hardly talked at all," wrote one of those who were with him at the end. " The look in his eyes had changed and he hardly ever could bring himself to laugh." His last utterance was characteristic. Watching his old father fussing helplessly around the bed, he murmured with a faint smile: " The old bastard!" On September 9, 1901, Lautrec passed away, at the age of 37, an age that has proved fateful for so many great artists.

AN EXAMINATION AT THE FACULTY OF MEDICINE, PARIS, 1901. (24¾×31″)
ON CANVAS. MUSÉE D'ALBI.

In a dimly lit room Gabriel Tapié de Céleyran is being put through the oral examination for his medical degree by Professors Wurtz and Fournier. The vivid red of gowns and faces shows up against a harmony of blacks and greens. The broad brushstrokes in these passages of red were a new departure, foreshadowing procedures we now associate with Rouault. Notable too is the hugeness of the hands, most meticulously delineated element of the composition.

LAUTREC AND HIS TIMES

LAUTREC defies classification in any of the well-known movements of his age, for he belonged to none. Yet instinctively he kept abreast of its most vital developments; for all that was new in art appealed to him. And in the same indirect manner he modified his contemporaries' way of viewing the world.

When he came to Paris the Impressionist group had almost wholly broken up. Lautrec admired Renoir and Monet, but Manet still more, because he had mingled more closely in the life of his day; temperamentally he felt nearer Degas and Whistler. Though a contemporary of the Neo-Impressionists and in contact with Seurat, Signac and Van Rysselberghe, he did not share their enthusiasm for theorizing about art; he much preferred Van Gogh's empirical achievements. None the less he read with interest Signac's *From Delacroix to Neo-Impressionism*. Lautrec picked up any hints that came his way, regardless of their source—from Princeteau, Raffaëlli and Forain no less than from the great masters. On two occasions he exhibited with the Impressionists and Symbolists; indeed Mellerio included him among the Symbolists. Actually all he had in common with them was an occasional use—in his posters— of the procedures of Cloisonnism.

Nor did he seek to influence others. Bonnard, Vuillard and Vallotton, all slightly younger than himself, admired his masterly drawing and the quickness of his eye, and Lautrec always regarded them as his equals. In fact he was " independent " in the exact sense of the word and had no wish to proselytize. Detesting as he did the " old gang," he exhibited

GEORGES ROUAULT (1871). COURT OF JUSTICE, 1908. (11¾×7¾")
WATERCOLOR. HAHNLOSER COLLECTION, WINTERTHUR.

▶

III

regularly only in the Salon des Indépendants. He refused to belong to any coterie and even to serve in a hanging committee.

His culture was profound, but masked by an ironical detachment. Only casual remarks, let fall without thinking, betrayed the fact that he had read widely and nothing lay outside his ken. Though he rarely visited art museums (the effort of walking through the rooms fatigued him), he showed a happy gift, when he did so, of discovering, after a hasty glance around, the work that appealed to him most and gave him what he was seeking for. Thus his friends tell of his gazing a full hour at a portrait by Cranach in the Brussels Museum, at a face by El Greco in the Prado, at Uccello's *Rout of San Romano* and a Baldovinetti portrait in the National Gallery, at Moïse de Camondo's Japanese prints.

For Lautrec only the figure counted, landscape was a mere accessory; Corot's greatness, to his thinking, lay solely in his figures and he regretted that Monet was so quick to give up figure painting. That impression of timeless validity we get from his paintings—though they are essentially the pictorialization of an epoch—is due to this obsession with the human figure and his feeling for its ever-changing, never-changing oneness. We can understand the influence he had on Picasso, who was quick to discern, surrounded as he was in his Barcelona days by the " modern style " imported from Munich and Paris, that here was an artist of complete integrity. True, the most typical themes of the *fin de siècle* were supplied by Lautrec, but more important was the lesson he gave of the magical power of linework, not only as drawing but as the vehicle of expressive color. Gustave Moreau used to tell his pupils to go and see a figure done by Lautrec " entirely in absinthe " as he put it, nor did they fail to do so: both the young Fauves who were soon to build form with color, and Rouault when he took to juxtaposing pigments flaring like molten metal.

SELECTED BIBLIOGRAPHY

EXHIBITIONS

INDEX OF NAMES

CONTENTS

SELECTED BIBLIOGRAPHY

Monographs and Appraisals

ESSWEIN & HYMEL, *H. de T. L.*, Piper, Munich 1909; reprinted 1916. — G. COQUIOT, *T. L.*, Blaizot, Paris 1913. — KLOSSOWSKI, *Die Maler von Montmartre*, Bard, Berlin 1914. — TH. DURET, *L.*, Bernheim-Jeune, Paris 1920. — ACHILLE ASTRE, *H. de T. L.* (preface by G. Geffroy), Nillson, Paris 1926. — MAURICE JOYANT, *H. de T. L.* (vol. I, paintings; vol. II, drawings, prints, posters), Floury, Paris 1926-1927. — P. DE LAPPARENT, *T. L.*, Rieder, Paris 1927; English translation, New York 1928. — F. FOSCA, *L.*, Druet, Paris 1928. — G. JEDLICKA, *L.*, Cassirer, Berlin 1929; re-issued, Zurich 1943. — P. MAC ORLAN, *T. L.*, *peintre de la lumière froide*, Floury, Paris 1934. — M. EXTEENS, *T. L.*, in *Dictionnaire Biographique des Artistes Contemporains*, Grund, Paris 1934. — GERSTLE MACK, *T. L.*, Knopf, New York 1938. — G. DE LA TOURETTE, *L.*, Skira, Geneva 1938. — J. LASSAIGNE, *T. L.*, Hypérion, Paris 1939. — J. RINALDINI, *T. L.*, Buenos Aires 1942. — L. BORGESE, *T. L.*, Hoepli, Milan 1945. — R. VON HOERSCHELMANN, *H. de T. L.*, Munich 1946. — F. JOURDAIN, *L.*, Marguerat, Lausanne 1948; *L.*, Braun, Paris 1951. — *T. L.*, Art Institute of Chicago, 1949. — M. G. DORTU, *T. L.*, Ed. du Chêne, Paris 1950. — F. JOURDAIN & J. ADHÉMAR, *T. L.*, Tisné, Paris 1952.

Reminiscences

PAUL LECLERCQ, *Autour de T. L.*, Floury, Paris 1920. — YVETTE GUILBERT, *La Chanson de ma vie*, Grasset, Paris 1927. — ARTHUR SYMONS, *From L. to Rodin*, John Lane, London 1929. — JANE AVRIL, *Mes Mémoires*, in Paris-Midi, August 7-26, 1933. — E. SCHAUB-KOCH, *Psychanalyse d'un peintre moderne*, *H. de T. L.*, Paris 1935. — F. JOURDAIN, *Né en 76, Souvenirs*, Paris 1951. — MISSIA, *Souvenirs*, Paris 1952. — THADÉE NATANSON, *Un H. de T. L.*, Cailler, Geneva 1952.

Books dealing with the drawings, prints and posters

LOYS DELTEIL, *Le peintre graveur illustré* (vols. X & XI, *H. de T. L.*), Paris 1920. — EDOUARD JULIEN, *Dessins de T. L.*, Documents d'art, Monaco 1942. — W. ROTZLER, *Les affiches de T. L.*, Holbein, Basel 1946. — CLAUDE ROGER-MARX, *Les lithographies de T. L.*, Hazan, Paris 1948. — MARIE DELAROCHE-VERNET-HENRAUX, *T. L. Dessinateur*, Quatre-Chemins, Paris 1949. — ED. JULIEN, *Les affiches de T. L.*, Sauret, Monte-Carlo 1950.

F. JOURDAIN, *L'affiche moderne et T. L.*, in La Plume, Nov. 1893. —
T. BERNARD, *T. L. sportsman*, in La Revue Blanche, May 15, 1895. —
G. GEFFROY, in La Vie artistique, 1900. — ROGER MARX, in La Revue
universelle, Dec. 13, 1901. — L. N. BARAGNON, *T. L. chez Péan*, in
La Chronique médicale, Febr. 15, 1902. — A. RIVOIRE, *T. L.*, in La Revue
de l'art, April 1902. — A. FONTAINAS, in Le Mercure de France, May &
June 1902. — H. FOCILLON, *L.*, in La Gazette des Beaux-Arts, June 1931.
— G. JEDLICKA, *L'écriture de L.*, in Formes, 1931. — A. LHOTE, in Parlons
Peinture, Denoël, Paris 1936. — R. HUYGHE, *Aspects de T. L.*, in La
Revue du Tarn, 1938.

Special numbers: Figaro illustré, April 1902. — L'Art et les artistes
(M. JOYANT), February 1927. — L'Amour de l'art (G. BAZIN, T. BERNARD,
R. COOLUS, R. HUYGHE, E. VUILLARD), April 1931.

Film: Toulouse-Lautrec, by ROBERT HESSENS, commentary by Assia
Lassaigne, Paris 1950.

EXHIBITIONS

Group exhibitions: Salon des Indépendants, Paris, 1889, 1890, 1891,
1892, 1893, 1894, 1895, 1897, 1902 (retrospective, 50 items), 1917, 1926.
— Cercle Volney, Paris, 1890, 1891, 1892. — Exhibitions of " Les XX "
and of " La Libre Esthétique," Brussels, 1892, 1893, 1894, 1895, 1896,
1897, 1902 (retrospective, 45 items). — " Exposition des peintres Impressionnistes et Symbolistes," Paris 1892, 1894. — Salon des Cent, Paris,
1895, 1896, 1897. — Salon d'Automne, Paris, 1904 (retrospective, 28 items).
One-man shows: Gal. Boussod & Valadon, Paris 1893. — Gal. Manzi
& Joyant, Paris 1896 — Lautrec's own studio, Avenue Frochot, Paris
1897. — Goupil Galleries, London 1897. — Gal. Joyant, Paris 1900. —
Gal. Durand-Ruel, Paris 1902 (200 items, preface by A. Alexandre). —
Gal. Barthelemy, Paris 1903. — Gal. Bernheim-Jeune, Paris 1908, 1936,
1948. — Musée des Arts décoratifs, Paris 1910. — Gal. Paul Rosenberg,
Paris 1914. — Gal. Manzi & Joyant, Paris 1914 (retrospective, 201 items,
preface by A. Alexandre). — Museum, Winterthur 1924 (preface by
G. Jedlicka). — Gal. Barbazanges, Paris 1924. — Gal. Wildenstein, New
York, 1925, 1946. — Art Institute, Chicago 1925, 1930, 1931, 1933. —
Musée du Luxembourg, Paris 1927 (lithographs). — Musée des Arts
décoratifs, Paris 1931 (423 items, preface by T. Bernard). — Gal. Knoedler,
New York 1937 (introduction by R. Huyghe & L. Carré); Paris 1938;
New York 1950. — Palais des Beaux-Arts, Brussels 1947. — Librairie
Michel, Paris 1948 (posters and lithographs). — Matthiesen Gallery,
London 1951 (66 items). — Musée de l'Orangerie des Tuileries, Paris
1951 (commemorating the 50th anniversary of Lautrec's death; 122 items,

preface by Michel Florisoone). — Bibliothèque Nationale, Paris 1951 (engraved work; 241 items, preface by Jean Vallery-Radot, notices by J. Adhémar). — Musée d'Albi, " Toulouse-Lautrec et ses amis," 1951 (183 items). — Venice Biennale, 1952 (lithographs from the Charrell Collection).

Inauguration of the Musée Toulouse-Lautrec at Albi, 1922 (catalogue with preface by Charles Géniaux; new edition by Edouard Julien, 1952, 500 items).

ILLUSTRATED BOOKS

Le Café-Concert, 22 lithographs (11 by Lautrec, 11 by Ibels), preface by G. MONTORGUEIL, L'Estampe originale, Paris 1893. — *Yvette Guilbert*, 16 lithographs, text by G. GEFFROY, Marty, Paris 1894. — *Portraits d'acteurs et d'actrices*, 13 lithographs, Paris 1895. — *Elles*, 11 lithographs, Pellet, 1896; reproduced by Mourlot, Sauret, Monte-Carlo 1952 — *Yvette Guilbert*, 11 lithographs, Blyss and Sands, London 1898; reprinted in 1930. — *Histoires naturelles*, lithographs, text by JULES RENARD, Floury, Paris 1899. — *Au cirque*, 22 facsimiles of color-crayon drawings dating from 1899, introduction by ARSÈNE ALEXANDRE, Manzi-Joyant, Paris 1905; 17 reproductions by Jacomet, Librairie de France, 1931; 37 reproductions by Mourlot, Sauret, Monte-Carlo 1952. — *70 Dessins de T.L.*, reproduced in facsimile, preface by M. JOYANT, Helleu and Sergent, Paris 1930. — *Yvette Guilbert*, 31 prints reproduced by Jacomet, introduction by C. ROGER-MARX, Le Pont des arts, Paris 1951.

INDEX OF NAMES

CONTENTS

THIS VOLUME
THE THIRD OF THE COLLECTION

THE TASTE OF OUR TIME

WAS PRINTED
BOTH TEXT AND COLORPLATES
BY THE

SKIRA

COLOR STUDIO
AT IMPRIMERIES RÉUNIES S. A.
LAUSANNE
FINISHED THE EIGHTH DAY OF MAY
NINETEEN HUNDRED AND FIFTY-THREE

PRINTED IN SWITZERLAND